Quotable Joe

Words of Wisdom by and about Joe Paterno, College Football's Coaching Icon

L. Budd Thalman

Foreword by Todd Blackledge

TowleHouse Publishing Company
Nashville, Tennessee

TowleHouse books distributed by Cumberland House Publishing, 431 Harding Industrial Boulevard, Nashville, Tennessee 37211.

Cataloging-in-Publication data
Thalman, L. Budd, 1935–
   Quotable Joe : words of wisdom by and about Joe Paterno / L. Budd
Thalman ; foreword by Todd Blackledge
     p. cm.
   Includes bibliographical references.
   ISBN 0-9668774-4-6 (alk. paper)
      1. Paterno, Joe, 1926---Quotations. 2 Football coaches--United States--
Quotations. I. Paterno, Joe, 1926- II. Title.

GV939.P37 T53 2000
796.332'092--dc21

                                                                    00-057694

Cover design by Gore Studio, Inc.
Page design by Mike Towle

Photographs courtesy of Mark Thalman, Tria Thalman, Steve Manuel, Penn State Sports Information, and Penn State University Photographics.

Printed in the United States of America

2 3 4 5 6—04 03 02 01

To my wife, Pattie,
the love of my life, my best friend, my greatest inspiration,
and to our three exceptional children,
Mark, Scott, and Kelly

Men are neither lions nor sheep. It is the man who leads them, who turns them into either lions or sheep.

—Jean Dutourd:
Taxis of the Marne, 1957

Contents

Quotable Joe

Introduction

Two things one should know about Joe Paterno. He is what he appears to be. And he doesn't take himself too seriously.

Like him, dislike him, Joe Paterno is the genuine article. He can be abrasive and is almost always outspoken, but he stands by his principles and doesn't take shortcuts to success. In a sport where there are plenty of temptations to bend the rules, Paterno stands steadfast in his resolve to do it the right way.

More than once, he has told Penn State boosters—who are less involved in the Nittany Lions athletic program than those at any other Division One institution in the nation—"We want your dollars, but we don't want your two cents!"

If you are around Joe Paterno for any length of time, he will charm you. He is sarcastic, informed, and funny, and he can laugh at himself. Once told that a student group was sponsoring a Joe Paterno look-alike contest, he said that he couldn't imagine "anyone wanting to win it."

He typically shakes his head when approached about another Joe Paterno product, like the golf balls with his image on them, which wags say will go up the middle three times out of four. He still can't get over the fact that people buy six-foot Paterno cutouts to take to weddings, birthday parties, alumni gatherings, and tailgates. One almost got arrested as an intruder when police were summoned after a neighbor saw the outline of a Standup Joe in the window of some vacationing neighbors.

One of my favorite Joe Paterno anecdotes recalls his first meeting with my father in 1986. My dad was a native West Virginian, a steel company foreman who sent his three children to West Virginia University and suffered through what seemed like centuries of Nittany Lions victories over the Mountaineers. When I went to work at Penn State, it was a bitter pill for him to swallow.

The night before the Penn State–West Virginia game at Morgantown in 1986, my sister brought my parents to the team hotel to attend a pregame reception in my suite that the coach typically dropped by to visit with the media, bowl representatives, and others. I introduced Mom and Dad to Paterno. Dad was on his best behavior.

Things were going smoothly until Dad happened to overhear Joe make a remark that got his Gold and Blue blood boiling. "Paterno," he roared from across the room, "you're full of (expletive deleted)."

While I was looking for cover and contemplating my next career move, Joe was across the room laughing heartily. I told the story in a eulogy when my dad died in 1998. Following the service, Joe said he wondered if I would remember his first meeting with my dad. How could one forget it!

Paterno's memory is epic and encyclopedic. It is impossible to recount the number of times I have seen him encounter former athletes, sometimes ten years after graduation, and not only remember their names but floor them by asking about their parents, "Frank and Sally." This from a man who has had several thousand players come under his influence in fifty seasons at Penn State.

At a Friday evening press gathering in 1998, we spoke about my return from a reunion of the 1963 Navy football team, which I was associated with as sports information director. Under the helmsmanship of Heisman Trophy winner Roger Staubach, the Midshipmen went 9-1 that season and played Texas in the Cotton Bowl in a dream matchup of No. 1 vs. No. 2.

Joe was in the stands that afternoon scouting Navy, which would open the 1964 season against Penn State. Top-ranked Texas took control of the game early with a pair of atypical long touchdown passes over a gimpy Navy defensive back. Thirty-five years later Paterno remembered the play. He took a napkin and diagrammed the Texas offensive formation like it had happened last week.

Paterno can talk to you about football, but he also can initiate conversations on politics, literature, economics, history, or just about any other subject you'd like to address.

This Renaissance man, however, can be contrary and intimidating. He can be in your face and on your case. A spot in Joe's doghouse is not something to which one aspires. Profanity is absent from his vocabulary, but he doesn't need it to make his point. The message arrives with a glare and an occasional high-pitched screech.

Joe Paterno realizes his faults, which is refreshing in a person of his fame and influence. For someone of his stature in the celebrity galaxy, he has less ego than anyone I've ever encountered. If you look for the ceremonial escort of state troopers on the Penn State sideline, you'll be disappointed. They're not there and they never have been.

If you're not around him every day, you can't imagine the demands for a piece of Joe Paterno. Corporations want him to make motivational speeches. The University wants him to do a fund-raising appearance. The Alumni Association wants him to visit a chapter meeting. A recruit's parents want him to discuss their son's college choice. Fans by the thousands want his autograph on footballs, books, photographs, and all kinds of memorabilia.

For fifty-one years, Joe Paterno has practiced a juggling act that rivals anything offered by Ringling Brothers and Barnum & Bailey. As his reputation has grown, several new balls seem to be added annually, but he continues to keep them in motion even as others his age are heading for rocking chairs on the front porch.

One of the things I find admirable about this icon of college football is that he hasn't lost his enthusiasm—for the kids, for the game, for the University, for life. He still gets up early every morning ready to attack the day—primed for whatever challenge awaits. As many times as he has assembled a game plan, or tinkered with a depth chart, or addressed a press conference, you would think he would find the routine boring. He doesn't.

The intrusions of his public persona on his football persona often are bothersome. To me, Joe Paterno is most at home between those white chalk lines on weekday afternoons and Saturdays, when he is consumed by the game that has been a passion since his Brooklyn childhood. Watching him prowl the practice field or the sideline on game day, one can almost hear his vigorous mind processing information. He has often admitted that Saturdays are the best of times—occasionally, although not often in his brilliant career, the worst of times.

"Legends have a confounding habit of showing up in strange places," *Sports Illustrated* columnist Rick Reilly wrote in an article that accompanied Paterno's selection as Sportsman-of-the-Year. "Two-hundred-eighty-pound linemen, college presidents, NCAA honchos, network biggies, and even your basic U.S. vice presidents cross-body-block one another to get near him. Good thing, too, because Joe Paterno, the football coach at Penn State University, can teach you some of the damnedest things."

Foreword

What is it like to play for Joe Paterno? If I had a dollar for every time I've been asked that question since I enrolled at Penn State in the fall of 1980, I'd be a wealthy man. The people I've met over the years, in football and outside of it as well, have a tremendous fascination with the person behind those trademark dark glasses.

Joe Paterno, the coach, has many defining characteristics, none more evident to me than his incredible consistency. Consistency of character, temperament, expectations, and standards is what makes Joe Paterno such a masterful coach and leader.

In my three seasons playing quarterback at Penn State, Joe and I did not always see eye to eye. We seemed to disagree most on the number of times we threw the football and the proper length of my hair. However, I never questioned where I stood with him or what he expected from me both on and off the field. I always felt that he dealt with me honestly, even when the outcome was not what I'd hoped for.

As Joe stands at the threshold of Bear Bryant's record for Division One victories, I can't help but feel that there isn't anyone in the long history of the game more deserving of being recognized as the best in the business than Joe Paterno. For fifty years, he has stayed the course. He has remained true to his principles. He has won with integrity. He has delivered on his promise of an education for the young men who have accepted his invitation to play for Penn State. He always has been a role model, never blinking in the face of opposition.

He has been Joe Paterno. Idealistic . . . Dedicated . . . Ethical—a man whose values, forged on the streets of Brooklyn and nurtured in the Ivy halls of Brown, anchor his football program in an often-turbulent sea. He's not someone to blind you with flash but a person who will win you over with honest sweat and genuine hard work.

As a proud product of Joe's program, I can tell you that virtually all of the players he's touched in fifty years as an assistant and head coach have been enriched by the experience. I consider myself, and I know my teammates and Penn State players past and present feel likewise, a better person for having played for Joe Paterno.

I always will regard it as a privilege to have been one of Joe's players and a singular honor to be the quarterback of his first National Championship team.

May he coach as long as his health permits. When he finally hangs them up, he'll walk hand-in-hand with the thousands of players who have come under his influence into the College Football Hall of Fame.

—*Todd Blackledge, CBS Television sportscaster and Nittany Lion*
quarterback for 1982 National Championship Team

Quotable Joe

1

Brooklyn and Brown

BY ALL ACCOUNTS, Joe Paterno lived an idyllic youth in Brooklyn, New York. Born on December 21, 1926, on 18th Street in the Flatbush section, Paterno was the first child of Angelo and Florence Paterno. The family later grew to include a brother, George, and a sister, Florence. Another brother, Frank, died in infancy.

Long before the days of organized youth sports, the Paterno brothers played in the street in an ethnic neighborhood, which included families of many nationalities. Joe still claims to have been a superior stickball player—a two-sewer man.

Joe was a Cub Scout, a Boy Scout, an altar boy, and an usher at Ebbets Field, where he formed an affection for the hometown Dodgers so deep that he still hasn't forgiven Walter O'Malley for taking the Bums out of Brooklyn.

After graduating from Saint Edmonds Grammar School, Joe and his brother George were enrolled by their parents in

Brooklyn Prep, a private Catholic school run by Jesuits. His father shouldered the tuition burden to see that his sons received the best possible education. It was at Brooklyn Prep that Joe began to thrive as an athlete and met the man, Father Thomas Bermingham, who challenged his intellectual instincts and created a lifelong interest in and respect for learning.

Joe was the quarterback and linchpin of the 1944 Brooklyn Prep football team that lost only once—to a Saint Cecilia High team coached by a young Vince Lombardi.

After being drafted into the army, Joe went to Korea following basic training. He was granted an early discharge in 1946 to play football for the Naval Academy. They're still waiting for him to take his oath as a Midshipman. Joe and his brother, George, instead headed for Providence, Rhode Island, home of Brown University.

Paterno played football and basketball at Brown. He was the heady quarterback of the Brown team that lost only once in nine games—to Princeton—in Joe's senior season. A teammate said his passes were hardly a thing of beauty, but he had no peers as a play caller.

I had a great childhood in Brooklyn.[1]

—*Paterno*

~

JOE WAS ALWAYS A CLASS ACT. HE WAS A GOOD HIGH SCHOOL
ATHLETE AND AN EXCELLENT SCHOLAR. HE NEVER HAD A BIG HEAD.[2]

—*Francis Mahoney, high school and college classmate*

~

HE WAS KIND OF A JOKESTER AND KIDDER, EXCEPT WHEN IT CAME
TO FOOTBALL. WHEN HE PLAYED FOOTBALL, HE ALWAYS SHOWED
HIS SERIOUS SIDE. HE WORKED HARD AT IT. ONE YEAR, HE LOST
THIRTY POUNDS. HE SCARED THE COACHES; THEY THOUGHT HE WAS
SICK, BUT HE STUDIED HARD AND KNEW THE GAME AS WELL AS ANY
OF THE COACHES.[3]

—*Martin Gresh, Brown teammate*

~

On reading Virgil's Aeneid *in Latin with Father Bermingham:*
I don't think anybody can get a handle on what makes me
tick as a person, and certainly can't get at the roots of how
I coach football, without understanding what I learned
from the deep relationship I formed with Virgil during
those afternoons and later in my life.[4]

—*Paterno*

~

AS WE BEGAN TO APPROACH ADOLESCENCE, THE PATERNO CHILDREN BECAME INTENSELY INTERESTED IN SPORTS. EVERYBODY PLAYED STICKBALL, ASSOCIATION, KICK THE CAN, BOX BALL, STOOP BALL, JOHNNY ON THE PONY, AND MARBLES IN THE STREETS. WE PLAYED BETWEEN PARKED CARS WITH A LOT OF MINOR TRAFFIC COMING UP AND DOWN THE STREET. WE PLAYED ENDLESSLY; IT WAS A GLORIOUS TIME.[5]

—*George Paterno*

PLAYING AS A SENIOR, JOE BECAME THE BRAINY QUARTERBACK. DICK REILLY, CHARLES WEISS, AND I WERE THE RUNNING BACKS. IT WAS AN OUTSTANDING SQUAD; SOME SAY THE BEST EVER AT OUR HIGH SCHOOL (BROOKLYN PREP). HOWEVER, WE DID LOSE ONE GAME. ACROSS THE RIVER IN ENGLEWOOD, NEW JERSEY, WAS A SCHOOL CALLED SAINT CECILIA'S. THEY HAD WON FORTY-SEVEN STRAIGHT GAMES, AND THE COACH'S NAME WAS VINCE LOMBARDI—LITTLE DID WE KNOW THE GREATNESS OF THE TEAM AND THE COACH WE LOST TO.[6]

—*George Paterno*

JOE DIDN'T PLAY AS A FRESHMAN (AT BROWN) BUT RIP ENGLE SAW SOME ATHLETIC SKILLS IN THIS BRIGHT, WIRY KID FROM BROOKLYN AND SO HE MADE HIM A DEFENSIVE BACK. BY THE END OF HIS PLAYING CAREER, JOE PROBABLY WAS REMEMBERED MORE FOR HIS DEFENSIVE SKILLS THAN HIS QUARTERBACK ACHIEVEMENTS. I THINK HE STILL HAS THE RECORD FOR INTERCEPTIONS.[7]

—*George Paterno*

HE CAN'T RUN, AND HE CAN'T PASS. ALL HE CAN DO IS THINK— AND WIN![8]

—*Stanley Woodward, Sports Editor*, New York Herald-Tribune

ALTHOUGH JOE CONSIDERED BASKETBALL TO BE HIS BEST SPORT, HIS COURT CAREER AT BROWN HAD ITS UPS AND DOWNS. IN HIS FRESHMAN YEAR, WEEB EWBANK WAS THE COACH AND JOE GOT HIS BIG CHANCE WHEN BROWN PLAYED A GREAT HOLY CROSS TEAM THAT WENT ON TO WIN THE NATIONAL CHAMPIONSHIP THAT YEAR. THE CRUSADERS WERE STOCKED WITH PROMINENT STARS, NOTABLY BOB COUSY—JOE FOUND HIMSELF PLAYING COUSY DURING THE GAME. COUSY, EVEN THEN A MASTER AT BALL-HANDLING, PASSING, AND SHOOTING, PRACTICED HIS LEGERDEMAIN ON THE YOUNG ROOKIE AND SCORED TWELVE POINTS IN ABOUT A MINUTE AND A HALF.[9]

—*Merv Hyman and Gordon White*, Football My Way

I grew up in Brooklyn and was an usher at Ebbets Field in the summer of 1943. I loved the Dodgers, with Hilda and her cowbell and with the Dodger "sym-phony." Many a year I yelled, "Wait 'til next year." All of my uncles (some of whom were immigrants), they were Yankee fans because of Lazzeri, DiMaggio, and Crosetti, and all of those guys. But, I was a Dodger fan—a diehard![10]

—Paterno

On his high school coach Earl Zev Graham:
He taught me what sportsmanship was all about—and (kept) things simple.[11]

—Paterno

IF YOU TOOK TWENTY GUYS FROM THE HIGH SCHOOL, PULLED THEM AT RANDOM, AND PUT THEM IN A ROOM TO BRAINSTORM ABOUT A THEORETICAL RECOMMENDATION FOR HOW TO RESHAPE AMERICA'S FOREIGN POLICY—I GUARANTEE YOU THAT JOE WOULD BE CHAIRING THE MEETING WITHIN FIVE MINUTES.[12]

—Joe Hurley, Brooklyn Prep classmate and teammate

On translating the Aeneid *from Latin as a high school student:*
WHAT WE DID TOGETHER ACTED AS A CONFIRMATION AND A CLARIFICATION FOR MUCH THAT WAS GOING ON IN HIMSELF AND HELPED CONFIRM WHAT HE ALREADY IN SOME SENSE WANTED TO BE DEEP DOWN. IF JOE HAD NEVER HAD THAT EXPERIENCE OF COPING WITH HIMSELF AS A YOUNG FELLOW WHEN I FIRST CAME TO KNOW HIM, I DON'T THINK (HE WOULD HAVE BEEN ABLE TO LEAD OTHERS).[13]

—Father Thomas Bermingham, teacher and mentor

I'VE COACHED BETTER RUNNERS AND BETTER PASSERS. I'VE NEVER COACHED A MORE HEADY QUARTERBACK. JOE WAS A REAL STRATEGIST. IN ADDITION, HE WAS AN INSPIRATIONAL PLAYER, THE TYPE WHO CAN CARRY A TEAM.[14]

—Rip Engle, Brown and Penn State football coach

JOE IS A TREASURE.[15]

—Father Thomas Bermingham

(JOE) WAS ALWAYS REALLY CORRECT ON A
MORAL POSITION. HE WAS ALWAYS THE VOICE OF
REASON—AND A HELL OF AN ADVERSARY. IN
THOSE CASES, WHERE HE FELT THERE WAS A
MORAL ISSUE (INVOLVED), HE WAS VERY
VOLATILE (AND) OUTSPOKEN.[16]

—Pat Flynn, Brown classmate

. . . can't run, can't pass; all he does is think and win.

2

Penn State

IT WAS NOT love at first sight. The street kid from Brooklyn found life in rural Central Pennsylvania so confining that he suggested to his coach, Rip Engle, that he might want to start looking around for a new assistant coach.

Fast-forward to the year 2000 and Joe Paterno obviously has found something to like. He has worked in the same department for fifty years, been married to the same wife for thirty-eight years, lived in the same house for thirty-one years, and been through untold pairs of white athletic socks.

He is Penn State's most recognizable citizen, every bit as representative of the University as Old Main or the Nittany Lions mascot. His image is on coffee mugs, sweatshirts, golf balls, and Christmas ornaments. It is impossible to mention Penn State without Joe Paterno coming to mind.

There is an ice cream named after him at the University creamery (Peachy Paterno), and the recently dedicated addition to the library is named the Paterno Library in honor of Joe and his wife, Sue, who chaired the fund-raising effort that underwrote its construction.

Joe has been active in a number of different campaigns to generate funds for University initiatives, including the present billion-dollar Grand Destiny drive.

He feels so deeply about the University that his family pledged $3.5 million, believed to be the most generous gift ever by a collegiate coach to a University, to endow faculty positions and scholarships and to support two building projects. "I find it truly remarkable," University president Graham Spanier said at the time of the 1998 contribution, "that Joe and Sue Paterno would take a substantial portion of their life savings and return it to the University."

Paterno always has encouraged Penn State's leadership to make the University as good as it can be. He candidly told the Trustees in a 1983 speech that they should undertake a major fund-raising initiative to get up the impetus needed to capture what he described as a magic moment in the institution's history.

"If I had an important role in development," he said, "it was in helping to change the whole mentality of giving. The whole idea of participation has changed at Penn State over the last ten years or so. More and more people are feeling an obligation to give, even if it's just a hundred dollars or so."

When I came here, I was determined we were going to have good football teams with people who belonged in college. People who could go out on a football field, knock somebody on their rear end, pick them up, not taunt then, and when they walked off that field, people who would be gentlemen, in some cases scholars, and be the kind of people everyone looked up to.[1]

—*Paterno*

On his initial reaction to State College:
After a few weeks, I told Rip, "I'm getting out of here before I go nuts in this town. You better start looking around for another coach."[2]

—*Paterno*

On the occasion of his family's $3.5 million contribution to Penn State:
Penn State has been very good to both Sue and me. We've met some wonderful people here, we've known many students who have gone on to become outstanding leaders in their professions and in society, and all of our children have received a first-class education here. I've never felt better about Penn State and its future potential than I do right now.[3]

—*Paterno*

On remaining at Penn State despite overtures to coach elsewhere:
A couple of times when we got licked I would think about why I didn't go back to law school. I have never had any regrets. I have been very, very fortunate with all of the decisions I have made in my life—where I went to school, deciding to take a chance on coaching here (at Penn State) with Rip Engle before going to law school, my selection of my wife, and the coaches I have been around. So I don't have any regrets.[4]

—*Paterno*

On his chances of getting the head-coaching job when Engle retired:
IF YOU'RE GOOD ENOUGH, YOU'LL GET THE JOB. THAT'S THE ONLY THING THAT'S GOING TO COUNT.[5]

—*Dr. Eric Walker, Penn State president*

On accepting the 1966 offer of $20,000 to be the head coach from Dean Ernie McCoy:
Holy smokes, that's super.[6]

—*Paterno*

I've said it a hundred times. A great library is the heart of a great university, and if we want to remain a big league university, we've got to have a big league library.[7]

—*Paterno*

On naming the new library wing after the Paternos:

SUE AND JOE PATERNO ARE LEGENDARY AT THIS INSTITUTION, NOT ONLY BECAUSE OF THE NOTABLE AND CONSISTENT SUCCESS OF THE NITTANY LIONS, BUT ALSO BECAUSE OF THE VALUES THEY HAVE ESPOUSED OVER THE YEARS. FAMILY, LEARNING, LOYALTY, AND COMMITMENT ARE PROMINENT AMONG THOSE VALUES. THIS NEW LIBRARY WILL STAND AS AN APPROPRIATE TRIBUTE TO ALL THAT THEY HAVE DONE FOR PENN STATE.[8]

—*Dr. Joab Thomas, former president of Penn State*

I've said this to a couple of people. It's not my line. This is the only school in the country where they build a basketball court (the Bryce Jordan Center) and they name it after a college president (Bryce Jordan) and they build a library and name it after the football coach.[9]

—*Paterno*

Joe and the Nittany Lions, ready to take the field.

Penn State has allowed me to be more than a football coach. The faculty here has always allowed me to be part of the faculty. My opinion was respected. I got into the mainstream of the intellectual community here. I've been included in a lot of things. If I just had to be the football coach here and be on the fringe of the University community, I never would have stayed. I would have been a pro.[10]

—*Paterno*

On ceremony celebrating his three hundredth coaching victory: You know, it's amazing. You think you know yourself. I didn't realize I'd get that choked up. It's been a great time. A great forty-eight years—We've been able to do well here because we've got people who are loyal to this institution and the administration has been loyal to them. We have people who come and they stay and bring up their families here and they make a commitment to this institution and its football program.[11]

—*Paterno*

On Penn State tradition:
I think the players are proud to wear those funny-looking uniforms and the black shoes. They came here with the idea they were going to play on a fine football team with a good tradition and I think they feel an obligation to that tradition.[12]

—*Paterno*

They ask me what I'd like written about me when I'm gone. I hope they write I made Penn State a better place, not just that I was a good football coach.[13]

—*Paterno*

We have a lot of people who enjoy football at Penn State. They enjoy the whole atmosphere and enjoy coming back. Sometimes, I am not sure if it is the football, tailgating, to see old friends, or to go downtown, but it is a happening. Penn State football—as is the case at Michigan, Ohio State, and many other places—is a happening. It's a reunion. It's a bunch of people coming together with a common cause. It's kind of fun these days to be able to join hands with fifty, sixty, or eighty thousand other people and all have the same thing in mind. It's something that people need. It's exciting to be around it.[14]

—*Paterno*

I think it (Penn State) is a great place to come because of the environment. Kids can come here and literally have a small-college atmosphere. I think the University has dramatically increased its prestige and quality of education with the faculty it has recruited. We have tried to keep our tuition reasonable. Kids come here and like it and pass the word on. We have very loyal Alumni—I think that anybody who comes here can sense the vibrancy of this place—This is not a stagnant University. This is a University whose future is ahead of it.[15]

—*Paterno*

3

College Athletics
and Academics

JOE PATERNO MAKES sure his athletes get a
meaningful education. "The purpose of
college football is to serve education, not
the other way around," he says.

The payoff to this emphasis on
academic excellence is reflected by a
football graduation rate that is consistently
among the best in Division One. In
Paterno's tenure, Penn State has had twenty-one first-team
GTE Academic All-Americans, fourteen National Football
Foundation and Hall of Fame Scholar-Athletes, and
seventeen NCAA Postgraduate Scholarship winners.

Paterno hasn't been hesitant to sit down players because
of academic deficiencies, often when they may have been
eligible by NCAA or Big Ten standards. The coach also has
encouraged his athletes to be involved in other activities, not

to become pigeonholed as just jocks. One of his former players, College Hall of Fame defensive lineman Mike Reid, was a pianist who was part of the cast for a campus production of *Guys and Dolls*. Reid now is a Grammy-winning singer-songwriter in Nashville.

His respect for education has led Paterno to take many positions on academic and eligibility standards for student-athletes, some occasionally unpopular. He has supported positive changes in the recruiting guidelines and is a long-time proponent for making freshmen ineligible. He is a vocal supporter of a stipend for student-athletes to permit them to be mainstream members of the college community.

For this son of Brooklyn, the title "coach" is not the one to be most prized. He is an educator first, a coach second.

I've had kids who didn't have a nickel in their pockets. I can't say, "Here is $100 until you get straightened out." I'm not for buying kids, but we ought to give them a decent scholarship. A lot of us are naive. There are academic scholarships available at Penn State and at most of the colleges in the country. Colleges will compete for the top-notch math or science student and give him or her room, board, books and tuition as well as clothing money, transportation money, what have you. That's not considered buying a student. If we give a football player a scholarship, it should be a decent one that enables him to buy an occasional pizza or go to a movie.[1]

—*Paterno*

I hound my players. "Don't let the world pass you by. Go after life. Attack it. Ten years from now I want you to look back on college as a wonderful time of expanding yourself—not just four years of playing football." All the more so if a kid's here on a football scholarship. I tell him, use it for more than just football. It's a ticket to the world. The purpose of college football is to serve education, not the other way around.[2]

—*Paterno*

HIS PHILOSOPHY WAS THAT COLLEGE WAS GETTING AN EDUCATION FIRST. I THINK WE ALWAYS FELT WE HAD SOMEONE SPECIAL IN JOE PATERNO. I WAS PART OF THE GRAND EXPERIMENT—THAT FOOTBALL PLAYERS CAN GET AN EDUCATION, THAT THEY CAN TALK, THAT THEY'RE NOT DUMB JOCKS.[3]

—John Skorupan, All-America linebacker (1970–72)

I don't think any committed coach can take issue with the involvement of the presidents in the administration of college athletics. At Penn State, we have had such institutional control and the participation of the presidents on the national level is indeed welcome. Having said that, I don't necessarily subscribe to all of the changes the President's Commission has instituted through the NCAA. Many reflect that our coaches and other athletic staff have not done a good job informing our presidents what constitute constructive changes. As a result, I am afraid we have created new rules and new restrictions which might diminish the coaches' ability to run athletic programs that are a source of personal growth and provide meaningful competition for our student-athletes.[4]

—Paterno

I really don't want a kid to leave here saying, "If they had gotten on my back a little more, I might have gotten a more meaningful education." I have been very fortunate that I had a great education. I appreciate it. People talk about my longevity. If I were honest with people, I feel that my education really made it possible for me to handle some situations that some other people haven't handled.[5]

—Paterno

On Title IX:
I think we have an obligation to give women the same kind of opportunities we give men. Having said that, I am concerned that there are people who want to take away from the men to give to the women. I don't think that is morally right either. I think the right thing to do is create more opportunities for women.[6]

—Paterno

4

Coaches and Coaching

AS THE CALENDAR turned to the year 2000, Joe Paterno was on the doorstep of the most precious college football record—total victories for a Division 1 coach. With 317 wins, only Bear Bryant (323 wins) and Pop Warner (319) stood between Paterno and the pinnacle.

Paterno is the winningest postseason coach of all time and has taken more teams to bowl games than anyone in the history of the profession. Penn State's win over Texas A&M in the 1999 Alamo Bowl was the twentieth bowl victory of Paterno's tenure and marked the thirtieth time he had put the Nittany Lions into the postseason.

He is the only coach to win the four traditional New Year's Day games—the Rose, Sugar, Cotton, and Orange Bowls. His teams are undefeated in five trips to the Fiesta Bowl.

His coaching resumé includes two National Championships (1982, 1986); five undefeated, untied teams; twenty finishes in the top ten of the national rankings; four

Coach-of-the-Year plaques; and more than 225 former players who made it to the National Football League, twenty-five of them first-round draft choices, including All-Americas Courtney Brown and LaVar Arrington, selected one-two in the 2000 NFL selection meeting.

His teams have registered seven undefeated regular seasons and he has had twenty-seven teams finish in the top twenty. Penn State has won the Lambert-Meadowlands Trophy, emblematic of Eastern Football supremacy, twenty-one times in Paterno's coaching run.

Since joining the Big Ten Conference in 1993, Penn State has the best overall record of any Big Ten team and the fifth-best mark nationally. In the fifty years Paterno has been associated with the program, the Nittany Lions have won 421 games and have a winning percentage of .759—tops in college football.

Paterno's decision to forsake law school to accept the invitation of Rip Engle, his coach at Brown, to join him as a rookie assistant coach at the then-Pennsylvania State College may have cost the nation a notable barrister, perhaps a judge of note, but it produced a college coach and educator without equal.

I think anybody who goes into college coaching these days is nuts. It is just so demanding. People expect you to be Moses.[1]

—*Paterno*

On staying in coaching:
My motivation has to come not only from what I want to do but also from my ability to get other people to do things the right way. If I have a strong suit, it's been the fact that I've set a standard.[2]

—*Paterno*

TWO OF PATERNO'S COACHING FOUNDATIONS WERE: FEAR ME MORE THAN ANY OPPONENT; RARELY WILL YOUR GAMES BE MORE PRESSURE-PACKED THAN YOUR PRACTICES.[3]

—*Ken Denlinger*, For the Glory

You've got to get better before you get perfect. We like to tell our football team: Do the little things right, and the big things will take care of themselves. Don't look for the touchdown all the time. Get in there tough, play after play, and then *boom*, all of a sudden a big play will present itself.[4]

—*Paterno*

What are coaches? Number one, we're teachers and we're educators. We have the same obligations as all teachers at our institutions, except we probably have more influence over our young people than anyone other than their families—we're dealing with emotions; we're dealing with commitment; we're dealing with discipline and loyalty, and pride. The things that make a difference in this life—pride, loyalty, and commitment—are the things that make a difference in this country. We need people to go out there and make a difference.[5]

—*Paterno*

I like to coach. I don't know whether it is just Penn State football but I like to coach. I enjoy the challenge of each particular season. I enjoy the challenge of trying to get different groups of guys together to play well. It's fun. I don't know how else to express it.[6]

—*Paterno*

I REALLY BELIEVE THAT WHEN JOE HANGS 'EM UP, HE MIGHT GO DOWN AS TOPS. I'M TALKING, WE CAN GO BACK TO ROCKNE, WE CAN GO BACK TO MY IDOL, BEAR BRYANT, GO BACK TO BOB NEYLAND, GO BACK TO ALL THE GREATS. JOE MIGHT BE THE GUY EVERYBODY LOOKS TO BECAUSE, TO ME, JOE HAS DONE EVERYTHING RIGHT. HE GRADUATES HIS PLAYERS, HE'S ARTICULATE, AND HIS CHARACTER IS IMPECCABLE, IN MY OPINION.[7]

—*Bobby Bowden, head football coach, Florida State*

FOR AWHILE, HE DID IT ALL. HE WAS THE ACADEMIC ADVISOR, THE OFFENSIVE COORDINATOR, THE DEFENSIVE COORDINATOR, AND CALLED EVERY PLAY AND EVERY DEFENSE. I DON'T KNOW THAT PEOPLE KNOW THAT. FROM PROBABLY 1967 THROUGH THE MID-70S, HE CALLED EVERY PLAY ON OFFENSE AND DEFENSE. HE DEVISED BOTH GAME PLANS. HE HAD THE DEFENSIVE GAME PLAN ON MONDAY AND THEN CAME IN WITH THE OFFENSIVE GAME PLAN ON TUESDAY.[8]

—*Fran Ganter, Penn State assistant coach*

I'VE LONG RESPECTED JOE PATERNO, NOT ONLY BECAUSE OF WHAT HE'S ACCOMPLISHED ON THE FIELD , BUT HE'S ONE OF THOSE GUYS WHO KEEPS GIVING BACK. YOU KNOW, THESE NCAA MEETINGS AND FOOTBALL COACHES' MEETINGS CAN BE VERY BORING. BUT JOE IS ALWAYS THERE, ALWAYS IN THE FRONT ROW, SPEAKING HIS MIND WHEN A LOT OF BIG NAMES IN OUR PROFESSION WON'T EVEN SHOW UP.[9]

—*Glen Mason, head football coach, Minnesota*

HE STILL DOES GASSERS WITH THE PLAYERS. BUT HE DOES THEM WITH THE OFFENSIVE LINEMEN. HE MOVED FROM THE SKILL PLAYERS TO THE LINEMEN.[10]

—*Tom Bradley, Penn State assistant coach*

On how his coaching style has changed over the years:
When I was a young coach, if we had a game televised
twice a year that was a big deal. You didn't have the
television people that wanted some time with you. You
didn't have press conferences twice a week. You had more
time. We didn't have as much information available to
you. You'd get three key films, one copy—Now we've got
videotapes coming out our ears. Every game is televised
and on the satellite. You go to your office and you're
locked in with tapes. You feel uncomfortable if you don't
look at a lot of them.[11]

—*Paterno*

I learned from Coach Bryant that I wasn't as good a coach
as I thought I was. He was a very interesting person to
coach against because he was so laid-back and would give
you a misleading appearance of what a fierce competitor he
was. He was really a gentleman. He was very soft-spoken.
His teams played with tremendous enthusiasm and were
very aggressive and very well organized.[12]

—*Paterno*

The last play isn't important. It's the next play that's important.[13]

—*Paterno*

I like young teams. I like the challenge of teaching them and coaching them.[14]

—*Paterno*

HE'S A STUDENT OF THE GAME. HE'S A GOOD COACH. JOE PATERNO IS GOOD FOR FOOTBALL.[15]

—*Woody Hayes, former head football coach, Ohio State*

On Paterno's decision to pursue a coaching career:
A COACH, YOU DIDN'T HAVE TO GO TO COLLEGE TO BE A COACH.[16]

—*Florence Paterno, Joe's mother*

Paterno has a postgame word for George Welsh, a Paterno assistant who went on to become head coach at Navy and Virginia.

We had a great series with Alabama in the 1980s and I remember before his first visit to State College in 1981, Coach Bryant placed a telephone call to me. I always had difficulty hearing him on the phone because of his slow, Southern drawl, and I was poised to pay special attention. He had learned about the two-hour bus ride from Harrisburg before and after the game and was concerned about sitting in postgame traffic. "Joe," he said, "I'm not as young as I used to be and I wouldn't look forward to a long bus ride following the game. Why don't you call the Governor and have him clear one lane, or arrange for us to drive on the shoulder, from State College to Harrisburg?" I told him, "Paul, I'm sure you could get that done in Alabama, but I'm not sure I can get it done in Pennsylvania!" I made the call but without the desired result.[17]

—Paterno

I WAS SURPRISED HE CHOSE COACHING OVER LAW. THEN IT DAWNED ON ME: HE'S GOING TO BE AN EDUCATOR. AND THAT'S WHAT HAS MADE HIM DISTINCTIVE AS A COACH. HE'S AFFECTING THE LIVES OF HIS PLAYERS. THEN IT DIDN'T SURPRISE ME ANYMORE.[18]

—Father Thomas Bermingham

That is what is nice about college coaching, it is never the same job two years in a row.[19]

—*Paterno*

About twenty years ago, we were sitting around at a little get-together and we got to arguing about coaching. I said something and Hayden Fry (the ex-Iowa coach) looked at me and said, "You don't know anything about coaching, Joe. You've never coached until you've been fired."[20]

—*Paterno*

A lot of people ask me why I don't wear headphones. The reason I don't is because I like to watch how the game is going so that if I see something that I think might help change it or keep up the pace, I am comfortable and not mixed up with a lot of details.[21]

—*Paterno*

You don't have to concern yourself with how a first-stringer feels. The real test is whether the last substitute has good morale. If he has, it means everybody has.[22]

—*Paterno*

To some coaches, graduation is disaster, the enemy. All the things I believe in force me to celebrate graduation as achievement, as victory. But a secret part of me weeps inside at commencement.[23]

—*Paterno*

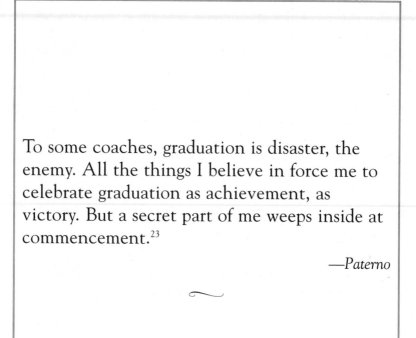

Football

A GOOD MEASURE of the success Joe Paterno has achieved as a football coach lies on the east side of the University Park campus of the Pennsylvania State University. It is the imposing superstructure of Beaver Stadium, soon to be the second-largest, on-campus facility of its kind in the nation.

Since Paterno took over the head-coaching responsibilities in 1966, Beaver Stadium has been expanded seven, count 'em, seven times. When the latest addition is complete for the 2001 football season, the Nittany Lions' lair will seat nearly 107,000. The football stadium was moved from the center of the campus to its current site in 1960, at which time it could accommodate 46,284.

Penn State has been playing to sold-out houses for as long as most can remember. A Penn State football ticket has become as valued as the bluest of blue-chip stocks.

There's nothing he enjoys more than football, Paterno allows. The game clearly energizes a man who appears far younger than his years. Paterno is not a tower coach, who observes drills from a tower on the practice field. He is actively involved, constantly making notes in his distinctive left-handed scrawl, correcting technique, checking alignment, sometimes even demonstrating.

Paterno values football's lessons of courage, dedication, judgment, a sense of team play, and a solid work ethic. He sometimes wonders, however, at what price. Major college football has become a year-round pursuit. He tries to keep the game in perspective for his players—to keep their feet solidly planted on the ground.

Football at Penn State is big-time. But the Nittany Lions still wear those vanilla uniforms, black shoes, emphasize defense and kicking, and don't strut or talk trash. Paterno has long preached that opponents are to be respected, not disdained. The fun of football, he says, is to try and beat the foe and to appreciate the fact he has given his best to try and beat you.

I'm not a guy that believes much in momentum or emotion. Football games are sixty minutes. The team that is the most disciplined, the most consistent, the one that hustles the most usually gets a break or two and usually wins the football game.[1]

—*Paterno*

I cannot adequately describe to you the love that permeates a good football team—a love of one another. Perhaps as one of my players said, "We grow together in love—hating the coach." But to be in a locker room before a big game and to gather a team around and to look at grown men with tears in their eyes, huddling close to each other—reaching out to be part of each other—to look into strong faces which say, "If we can only do it today"—to be with aggressive, ambitious people who have lost themselves in something bigger than they are—this is what living is all about.[2]

—*Paterno*

Football isn't a very complicated game if you don't get penalized, don't turn the ball over, and don't make mistakes in the kicking game.[3]

—*Paterno*

On speed in football:
Speed has changed the game. There's not much question
that if the other fellow has fast players you need them to
stay close to him. Either that or you had better make the
field shorter and narrower.[4]

—*Paterno*

If you aspire to be a good football team, you have to be able
to overcome yourself. You have to be able to overcome the
team playing against you, and you have to be able to
handle the elements. It's not like basketball, where you
play in a warm gym all the time or baseball where if the
weather is bad you cancel the game.[5]

—*Paterno*

Football is a great game. It demands a young man's total
commitment—emotionally, mentally, and physically. It
challenges our young people to do their very best, to
discipline themselves to develop mental, as well as physical,
toughness. At its best it is a wonderful and worthwhile
experience, which will have immense future character
benefits for its players.[6]

—*Paterno*

Football is not the most important thing in this country. If football suddenly disappeared from the scene tomorrow, we would never miss it. European countries get along without it and they still exist.[7]

—*Paterno*

I figure that football has two seasons. First, there is the pre-season practice. We have about ten dog days when the players work their tails off and maybe even wonder why they ever got involved in this crazy game. I think we probably work them harder than anybody else in the country. Then, after that is over, we want to get the kids rested up so they can enjoy the season. After all, they are only going to play about thirty college football games in their lifetime and they ought to enjoy them.[8]

—*Paterno*

If we could get that feeling—that "we" and "us" instead of
"I" and "me"—into our society we wouldn't have as many
problems and we would be able to lick those we have.
Maybe we can't solve the national problems, but I think
that if we can make it work on the level of a football team,
maybe some of it will spill over onto the campus, and
maybe from the campus to the community, from the
community to the county, from the county to the state, and
from the state to the nation. But people have to work at it.[9]

—*Paterno*

When we didn't have face masks, we didn't have a lot of
holding. If you held a guy, he would punch you right in the
mouth. The worst thing we have right now are the helmets.
If you took the face mask off the helmet, added a single slim
bar and made it lighter, you wouldn't have as many knee
injuries. You wouldn't have guys out there killing each
other. You would go back to shoulder blocking. Right now
the helmet is a weapon.[10]

—*Paterno*

I think you go out there to play to win and respect your opponent. You are not out there to embarrass him. You try to beat him and appreciate the fact he has given his best to try and beat you. Otherwise, there wouldn't be any fun in playing. I don't think there is any need to embarrass anybody. I am not going to let the polls or public sentiment affect what I think a good tough football game should be all about. That is to win it, not to embarrass anybody.[11]

—*Paterno*

I didn't exactly play in the biggest league (the Ivy League at Brown) in the world but it was fun any time you played.[12]

—*Paterno*

Basically, I would still prefer to be able to go into a football game and be able to control it with our defense and kicking and not have the offense make a lot of mistakes.[13]

—*Paterno*

On sportsmanship:
I have a sense that it is starting to come back. Kids are starting to appreciate each other a little bit more and show more respect for each other. I don't see as much of the things that really bothered me like trash talk and that kind of stuff. You see more people picking each other up. You don't see kids taunting.[14]

—*Paterno*

We know more about how to throw the ball in college than we used to know. We have better indoor facilities so we can actually have the kids throw the football all winter as opposed to the old days . . . Once we started to build good indoor facilities, it was possible to be competitive with the passing game.[15]

—*Paterno*

Football is not a very complicated game. You can probably pick it up easier than most other games if you have certain basic skills. If you have good vision, good feet, can catch the ball, and have quick hands to get rid of it. Obviously, when you start getting into the bigger positions, strength, courage, and those things come into it.[16]

—Paterno

As I have said many times for a team to become excellent it has to overcome individual preferences and individual performances.[17]

—Paterno

Football can be an intellectual exercise and I want people who will think about what we can do and not be content to rubber-stamp my thoughts or be satisfied with what has worked in the past.[18]

—Paterno

Penn State quarterback Chuck Burkhart gets instructions from Paterno.

On the opinion that he's the conscience of college football:
I think maybe just because I have been at it longer than a lot of people and the type of program we run has been sound and solid may have impressed some. Hopefully, we've operated within the rules. Penn State's success has given me a little more visibility than some other people, but I don't consider myself the conscience of college football.[19]

—*Paterno*

6

Game Day

 IN A 1995 SURVEY conducted by the Long Island daily newspaper *Newsday*, Paterno was voted No. 1 as the best head coach at preparing his team for Saturday. The Penn State record substantiates *Newsday*'s conclusion. The Nittany Lions coach once spoke of the contemporary who said he liked everything about the profession but Saturday. "I live for Saturdays", was Paterno's response.

To watch him burst out of the South end zone tunnel running ahead of the blue and white-clad behemoths behind, one can't help but see a man energized by his vocation. He clings to the past by continuing to wear a coat and tie on the sidelines, when most of his contemporaries have gone to jackets and polo shirts. He disdains wearing a headset because he prefers to get a feel for the game without the distraction of conversation with the press box. He never wears a hat no matter how severe the weather.

The day has passed when he called every offense and every defense. He can't detach himself to the point, however, that he doesn't take over the play calling for a while in tense moments. His reputation for playing it close to the vest is often challenged by daring gambles. He will forever be remembered for a fourth-and-one call at his own fifteen-yard-line in a Gator Bowl game with Florida State that the Lions led at the time, 17-0. The gambit backfired and the Seminoles came back to tie, 17-17.

In a game against top-ranked Notre Dame at South Bend in 1990, the Monday morning quarterbacks wailed when he punted with 2:15 to play and the score tied. The wisdom of his decision emerged on the ensuing defensive series when Penn State intercepted the frantic Irish and kicked a field goal for a memorable 24-21 upset.

Thorough planning and precise practices make game day a tasty dessert. Paterno constantly tells his athletes to enjoy the games, to consider the pressure and the hard work behind them. It is a philosophy that has paid off with victory more than three hundred times since he ascended to the coach's chair in 1966.

On encountering Paterno on his walk to Beaver Stadium:
JOE PATERNO LIVES ON THE NORTH SIDE OF STATE COLLEGE, PERHAPS A MILE OR SO FROM THE STADIUM, AND HE IS IN THE HABIT OF WALKING TO THE DRESSING ROOM BEFORE THE GAME. AS YOU ARE LINED UP IN TRAFFIC, THE LAST PERSON YOU EXPECT TO SEE IS THE HEAD FOOTBALL COACH. I AM SURE THAT MOST FANS WOULD THINK HE IS IN A STAFF MEETING, MAKING FINAL CHANGES TO THE GAME PLAN OR SOMETHING. BUT THERE HE WAS, WALKING ALONG THE ROAD.

ALMOST AS IF A MAGIC SIGNAL WAS PASSED, CAR WINDOWS WERE ROLLED DOWN, PEOPLE BEGAN TO GREET JOE AT THE CURB, AND FANS BEGAN TO HAND OUT PIECES OF PAPER OR GAME PROGRAMS, HOPING TO GET JOE'S AUTOGRAPH. HE WAVED, SMILED, AND CROSSED THE ROAD RIGHT IN FRONT OF OUR CAR.

AS SOON AS HE RECOGNIZED US AND BEGAN TO WAVE, I ROLLED DOWN THE WINDOW AND ASKED, "ARE YOU GOING TO THE GAME?" "WHAT GAME?" THEN THE CONVERSATION TOOK OFF SOMETHING LIKE THIS:

ME: "PENN STATE IS PLAYING PURDUE TODAY."

JOE: "IS IT GOING TO BE A GOOD GAME?"

ME: "IT BETTER BE. IF PENN STATE DOESN'T WIN TODAY, THEY MAY FIRE THEIR COACH."

JOE: "I THOUGHT HE HAD A GOOD RECORD."

ME: "HE DOES, BUT PENN STATE FANS ARE SPOILED. THEY DON'T LIKE TO LOSE."

JOE: "WHAT TIME DOES THE GAME BEGIN?"

ME: "1:30."

JOE: "I'LL TRY AND MAKE IT!"[1]

—*Mickey Bergstein, former Penn State broadcaster*

To his 1990 squad on playing the Fighting Irish in Notre Dame Stadium:
Knute Rockne won't be out there to put a spell on you. The Four Horsemen aren't going to be around. Nobody's going to put a curse on you. I don't believe in ghosts so you shouldn't believe in ghosts. The best eleven will win.[2]

—*Paterno*

We work hard to achieve our goals and when Saturday comes and we walk on the grass in this stadium, we stand as a team. We tighten up our belts. We look across at our opponents. We say, come on, let's go, let's see how good you are, let's play. We are ready. We play with enthusiasm and recklessness. We aren't afraid to lose.[3]

—*Paterno*

On his first game as head coach:
I was scared to death. It was probably as poorly coached a college football game as you ever saw. We won the game because Mike Reid created three safeties by himself. Lou Saban was the coach at Maryland. He had just left the American Football League where he had won the championship at Buffalo. He left because he was tired of pro football and wanted to try college. This was his first game at Maryland—After the game was over, I ran over to see Lou. I didn't know what coaches said after a game and I couldn't find Lou. I felt a little bit dejected. I went home and he called me on Monday and said, "I apologize for not coming over to congratulate you, but we were both so lousy I didn't have the heart to congratulate anybody."[4]

—*Paterno*

No football game is the same. They may seem that way; they are not. And the preparation for each is different.[5]

—*Paterno*

Playing the game on Saturday is when we have our fun. That's when all the hard work pays off. The fun is to be relaxed, to be loose, just to play as if it's a sandlot game. We tell our players, "Don't worry about losing. Just relax and do your best. Enjoy it."[6]

—*Paterno*

A game plan should include only as many plays as you can practice well. More than half the time, a coach brings a game plan that is too big and fat with too many offensive plays, too many defensive plays. We struggle to practice all of it and we leave too much of it not practiced well enough. In a sixty-minute game, you can't afford to have a single play that is not practiced to perfection. That is far more important than razzle-dazzling the opponent with clever surprises.[7]

—*Paterno*

Nobody coaches a perfect game and nobody plays a perfect game—There are 160 decisions that have to be made, maybe more, in a football game. They have to be made within twenty-five seconds. When you have to make that many, with that kind of pressure, you are going to make some mistakes.[8]

—*Paterno*

I enjoy Saturdays and the football games. I enjoy the competition. I enjoy being around young people.[9]

—*Paterno*

I once went into the Green Bay locker room with my high school coach when (Vince) Lombardi was with the Packers. He was walking back and forth puffing on a cigarette. My coach said to him, "Do you still get nervous before a game?" Lombardi said, "If I don't get nervous I'm going to get out of it." I think all of us (coaches) are in the same boat. I will be nervous before we kick off. When we kick off, I will be involved in the game and the nervousness will be gone.[10]

—*Paterno*

There are few things that people will do in their lives that sixty thousand people will cheer them for.[11]

—*Paterno*

THE HARDEST WE PRACTICED WAS FOR A TEAM HE KNEW WE COULD BEAT, 70-0, AND WE KNEW WE COULD BEAT, 70-0. THE TEAM HE KNEW WE WOULD HAVE A ROUGH TIME WITH HE WOULD SAY, "OKAY GUYS, LET'S RELAX."[12]

—*Greg Buttle, All-America linebacker (1973–75)*

7

The Players

JOE PATERNO HAS admitted that the Penn State football program isn't for everyone.

He is a demanding taskmaster. High-profile athletes, many accustomed to kid-glove treatment, rebel at the discipline he requires. No hats in the house . . . walk on the sidewalk not the grass . . . no earrings . . . jackets and ties on road trips—all Paterno rules that seem old-fashioned in today's "anything goes" environment.

Meetings at Penn State convene on Paterno time, which is ten minutes ahead of schedule—sometimes more.

When they look back on their Penn State football experience, former players have a common perspective on the coach's long-term objectives for them. Former defensive lineman Matt Millen, now a broadcaster for Fox Sports, said: "Kids who stay in his program mature and get an idea of what life is about. Very few go into his program and come out at the same level they went in, and that's as a player and as a person."

Paterno respects dedication and commitment, which are reflected in his loyalty to players who have, in his words, "paid their dues." And, he can show a compassionate side as was demonstrated in a 1973 game that involved Heisman Trophy winner John Cappelletti. Cappelletti's brother, Joey, was battling terminal leukemia. Prior to the West Virginia game, Joey asked John to score four touchdowns against the Mountaineers—something he'd never done previously. Cappy was well on his way to delivering on his promise, scoring three times before Paterno lifted him from the game with Penn State comfortably in control. The coach had no wish to run up the score on an outmanned opponent.

Co-captain Mark Markovich, who had overheard Cappelletti's conversation with his brother, approached Paterno on the sideline and whispered something in his ear. The coach turned, gestured to Cappelletti, and sent him back into the game. Minutes later, Cappy delivered on his promise to Joey by bursting into the end zone for a fourth touchdown.

JOE PATERNO MASS PRODUCES MEN.[1]
                        —*Dave Robinson, All-America end (1960–62)*

On life with Paterno:
LIKE PLAYING FOR YOUR DAD IN A BAD MOOD.[2]
                        —*John Gerak, offensive lineman (1989, 1991–92)*

On selecting Paterno to present him for induction into the Pro Football Hall of Fame:
THE REASON JOE PRESENTED ME IS BECAUSE WHEN YOU'RE AN EIGHTEEN- OR NINETEEN-YEAR-OLD KID GOING TO COLLEGE, YOU CAN GO IN A LOT OF DIFFERENT DIRECTIONS. JOE GOT ME GOING THE RIGHT WAY. HE MADE SURE I REALIZED THAT IT WAS YOUR EDUCATION, YOUR FAMILY, AND THEN FOOTBALL. I LIKE THE WAY HE RAN HIS PROGRAM—NO ATHLETIC DORMS, HE DIDN'T MAKE FOOTBALL PLAYERS BIGGER THAN LIFE. HE MADE ME REALIZE THAT FOOTBALL WAS NOT THE MOST IMPORTANT THING IN MY LIFE. I WAS FORTUNATE TO BE IN HIS PROGRAM FOR FOUR YEARS. IT TOOK ME ABOUT FIVE SECONDS TO DECIDE ON JOE PATERNO TO PRESENT ME.[3]
                        —*Jack Ham, All-America linebacker (1968–70)*

Linebacker Jack Ham paid Paterno a great tribute by asking his college coach to present him at his induction into the Pro Football Hall of Fame.

JOE PATERNO IS A GOOD GUY. NOT THE TYPE TO PUT HIS ARM AROUND YOU, NOT THE TYPE WHO JOKES WITH YOU, BUT THE TYPE WHO HELPS YOU, FORCES YOU TO DEVELOP TO YOUR FULLEST POTENTIAL.[4]

—Bob White, defensive lineman (1983–86)

PEOPLE SEE HIS AGE BUT HE DOESN'T ACT AS OLD AS HE IS. IT'S PHENOMENAL WHAT HE CAN DO AT HIS AGE. HE IS SO GOOD AT DEALING WITH PEOPLE. HE RELATES WELL TO PLAYERS, EVEN THOUGH TIMES HAVE CHANGED. FOOTBALL HAS CHANGED SO MUCH OVER THE YEARS, BUT HE HAS BEEN ABLE TO CHANGE WITH IT. WHEN THEY JOINED THE BIG TEN, THAT WAS GOING TO BE A DIFFERENT STYLE OF FOOTBALL FROM WHAT THEY WERE USED TO. BUT HE WAS ABLE TO ADAPT THERE, TOO.[5]

—Aaron Gatten, linebacker (1997–98)

WE TALK ALL THE TIME. THAT GUY WHO JUST GOT DONE REAMING US OUT IS SEVENTY-TWO YEARS OLD. HE'S AS OLD AS MY GRANDMOTHER, AND SHE'S REALLY SICK. I JUST HOPE I'M BLESSED AND THAT FORTUNATE TO BE AS VIBRANT AND AS USEFUL AS HE IS WHEN I'M THAT OLD.[6]

—Brandon Short, All-America linebacker (1996–99)

The main thing Joe gives you is perspective. He's a teacher. He does more than football stuff. He's always giving you these little speeches, and after awhile you hear them so often and understand them and they're pretty true.[7]

—*Matt Millen, All-America defensive lineman (1976–79)*

When you think of putting your mark on life, there are very few people you look at and say, "He is that." But he's Penn State.[8]

—*Chuck Burkhart, quarterback (1968–69)*

I learned to stand up for myself well because of the things I was taught being around him.[9]

—*Lydell Mitchell, All-America tailback (1969–71)*

IT IS COMMONLY STATED THAT A FOOTBALL TEAM TAKES ON THE PERSONALITY OF ITS HEAD COACH. I THINK THAT IS PARTICULARLY TRUE OF PENN STATE TEAMS. NITTANY LIONS SQUADS THROUGHOUT THE YEARS (WITH A FEW EXCEPTIONS) HAVE BEEN CONSISTENTLY PHYSICAL TEAMS WHO ARE FUNDAMENTALLY SOUND AND DO NOT BEAT THEMSELVES. THAT CONSISTENCY STARTS AT THE TOP WITH JOE PATERNO.[10]

—*Todd Blackledge, quarterback (1980–82)*

I'VE ALWAYS HAD A GOOD RELATIONSHIP WITH JOE, BUT I HAD MY MOMENTS. I THINK EVERYBODY DID WHEN JOE PUSHED US. BUT I NEVER FELT THAT JOE WASN'T TRYING TO GET US TO BE THE BEST PLAYERS WE COULD BE.[11]

—*John Cappelletti, Heisman Trophy–winning running back (1971–73)*

HE LETS HIS PLAYERS CALL HIM BY HIS FIRST NAME, A RADICAL DEPARTURE FROM THE TRADITIONAL PLAYER-COACH PROTOCOL. "BETTER THEY CALL ME JOE THAN SOMETHING ELSE," HE REASONS.[12]

—*Merv Hyman and Gordon White*, Football My Way

The definition of a good football player is not only physical ability. It is the ability to do certain things under a lot of pressure.[13]

—Paterno

IF YOU SAT DOWN WITH JOE FOR FIVE MINUTES, HE COULD MAKE YOU FEEL GOOD, LIKE YOU WERE WALKING ON AIR AFTER YOU LEFT THE OFFICE.[14]

—Richie Lucas, All-America quarterback (1957–59)

Young people today are under so much pressure from so many different things that we never had (as youngsters)— the pros, the agents, the drugs, the exposure, and television. They have to be so straight. . . . I think coaches today have a large burden to keep them (the athletes) focused on the fact that they are in college to get an education, help them adjust to some things, help them to find out who they are and what is important in their lives, what is going to make them successful and what is going to make them happy. I think those things are all vital in the relationship between a coach and a player.[15]

—Paterno

AFTER A GUY HAS PLAYED FOUR OR FIVE YEARS FOR HIM, HE WALKS
OUT OF STATE COLLEGE AND PROBABLY SAYS, 'WHAT A JERK.' AS
THEY MATURE, THAT'S WHEN THEY COME TO APPRECIATE WHAT JOE
IS ALL ABOUT. A LOT OF KIDS ARRIVE THINKING THEY'RE STARS AND
WILL GO RIGHT TO THE PROS AND THE HALL OF FAME, UNREALISTIC
GOALS. BUT KIDS WHO STAY IN HIS PROGRAM MATURE AND GET AN
IDEA OF WHAT LIFE IS ABOUT. VERY FEW GO INTO HIS PROGRAM AND
COME OUT AT THE SAME LEVEL THEY WENT IN, AND THAT'S AS A
PLAYER AND AS A PERSON.[16]

—*Matt Millen, All-America defensive lineman (1976–79)*

On walk-on (nonscholarship) players:
Walk-ons are always going to be a very important part of
our program. They have to be, particularly now with
eighty-five grants. I always try to keep a scholarship or two
available in case somebody comes in and is better than
players we've recruited. You need them because they help
you practice. Some of them get to be better football players
than others. Almost all of the walk-ons are the most loyal
people we have. They are not looking, in most cases, for
what they can get out of it. They just want to be a Penn
State football player, part of the program and proud of it.[17]

—*Paterno*

HE HAS THE EYES OF AN EAGLE. HE COULD SEE THROUGH TREES,
AROUND CORNERS, THROUGH PEOPLE. IF YOU WERE DOING
SOMETHING WRONG, YOU COULDN'T HIDE. I NEVER FIGURED OUT
HOW HE DID IT.[18]

—Dave Joyner, All-America tackle (1969–71)

I DON'T THINK JOE ASKS TOO MUCH OF HIS PLAYERS. TO PLAY THIS
GAME, YOU HAVE TO BE MENTALLY TOUGH, AND THE ONLY WAY TO
BECOME MENTALLY TOUGH IS TO BE PUSHED. WHEN IT HAPPENS,
THEY THINK THEY'RE BEING ABUSED. THERE'S A DIFFERENCE
BETWEEN BEING PUSHED AND BEING ABUSED. THERE'S A LINE AND,
PERSONALLY, I DON'T THINK JOE OVERSTEPS IT.[19]

—Dennis Onkotz, All-America linebacker (1967–69)

HE WANTS TO CREATE PEOPLE WHO WILL COME OUT OF THIS
INSTITUTION AND WILL CONTRIBUTE GREATLY TO SOCIETY AND WILL
HAVE LEARNED A GREAT DEAL ABOUT LIFE.[20]

—John Shaffer, quarterback (1984–86)

IF YOU'RE NOT A MAN WHEN YOU GET HERE,
YOU'LL BE A MAN BEFORE YOU LEAVE. SO THIS IS
A GREAT PROGRAM FOR THAT. AND MAN, IT
WILL TEST YOU MENTALLY—AT TIMES, IT WAS
TOUGH, BUT THAT'S JUST BECAUSE OF THE WAY
JOE HAS HIS SYSTEM SO THAT YOU'RE PREPARED
FOR LIFE. JOE TRAINS YOU MORE MENTALLY
THAN PHYSICALLY, SO THAT NOTHING WILL
RATTLE YOU.[21]

— *LaVar Arrington, All-America linebacker (1997–99)*

8

Winning and Losing

THERE WAS A point when Joe Paterno had some doubt he would ever be a successful college football coach.

After a 5-5 rookie season in 1966, the Nittany Lions lost the opening game of the 1967 campaign to Navy 23-22 in Annapolis. "Our team played the shabbiest football game I had ever been part of," Paterno said in his autobiography. After the first eleven games of his career, the new Penn State mentor was an unexpected 5-6.

"After that game I felt, for the first time, concerned about my future as a coach," Paterno recalled. "I wondered whether I really had it. There were doubts in my mind—It just had never dawned on me prior to that game that I wasn't going to be a real good football coach, or that I couldn't be a good football coach. But now, out of a clear blue sky, I'm in trouble."

On the long bus ride home, Paterno pondered the changes that had to be made, including sitting down some

veteran players to make way for some more talented but less experienced youngsters.

A week later in Miami, against a strong Hurricane football team, Paterno began making substitutions early and, by the end of the first period, had practically a whole new team on the field. The Nittany Lions won, 17-8. After a loss to UCLA the following week, Penn State embarked on a streak of thirty-one games without a loss, including three bowl games. It was a streak that didn't end until the second game of the 1970 season.

Paterno's bout of self-doubt proved ill-founded. In the intervening years, he has won nearly 80 percent of the games his teams have played. He has won a record number of bowl games to go along with the national championships, Eastern championships, a Big Ten championship, and he has had teams finish in the top twenty of the national polls twenty-seven times in thirty-two years.

The decisions on that bus ride back from Annapolis laid the foundation for what has become one of the most successful college programs in the history of the game.

I just hate to lose. I know I preach a lot about being willing to lose, that there can be valor in losing to a better opponent, but I have never learned how not to hate losing.[1]

—*Paterno*

Winning is a matter of knowing how to win—part of being a Penn State player is knowing how to win. I'm not just talking about football. Anything. If this is what I want to do I can and I will.[2]

—*Paterno*

Just winning is a silly reason to be serious about a game. For a kid still in school, devotion to winning football games at nearly any cost may cripple his mind for life. Institutions of higher learning don't have the moral right to exploit and mislead inexperienced kids that way.[3]

—*Paterno*

On winning three hundred games:
I never thought I would get to one hundred—I never
thought I would stay in coaching that long. Anybody who
figures on staying in it as long as I have has got to be a
little kooky, and maybe that explains it.[4]

—*Paterno*

I think there's no question that having a winning tradition
and understanding what it takes to win is a plus. On the
other hand, at times you can get careless when you're used
to winning. You don't realize what it took to win and you
forget little things. Jerry Kramer wrote an article in *Sports
Illustrated* when the Packers started to have some problems.
I think he called it "Death by Inches." There is a thin line
between being confident and being stupid.[5]

—*Paterno*

Success without honor is an unseasoned dish, it will satisfy
your hunger but it won't taste good.[6]

—*Paterno*

I have never walked away from a football game that we lost that I felt that I couldn't have done a better job.[7]

—*Paterno*

⌒

I always remember what Winston Churchill once said: "Success is never final, failure never fatal." I think maybe that best explains my philosophy of football as well as life in general.[8]

—*Paterno*

⌒

On losing at Colorado to end a thirty-one-game unbeaten streak: The trip wasn't a total loss, though. My wife got to see the Rockies.[9]

—*Paterno*

⌒

More on losing at Colorado:
There's an elation to winning and when you get beaten too often you get angry. But when you haven't lost in a long time you find out just how ignominious it is. But look at me, I've finally acquired character. That feels good.[10]

—*Paterno*

The best man, the best team, isn't automatically entitled to win. The winds of fate can turn you around, run you aground, sink you, and sometimes you can't do a thing about it. You can commit yourself to accomplishing a goal, doing something good, winning a game. Just to make that commitment to something you believe in is winning—even if you lost the game. But for committing yourself to winning the game, whether you win it or not, you always pay in tears and blood.[11]

—*Paterno*

I've said many times that you're never as good as you look when you win, and you're never as bad as you look when you lose.[12]

—*Paterno*

I don't think anybody fears a loss. If you are in this game and you're going to go out there and are afraid to get licked, then you are in the wrong business. After all of these years, I hope that's not what people think about the way we approach a football game.[13]

—*Paterno*

On being uncomfortable in press conferences following a victory:
I have empathy for the other team.[14]

—*Paterno*

9
National Championships, Polls, and Publicity

WHEN IT COMES to evaluating the usefulness of college football polls, Joe Paterno qualifies as perhaps the ultimate expert.

In his thirty-four seasons as head coach at Penn State, he has had four different teams finish undefeated and unappreciated. The 1968 and 1969 Lions posted identical 11-0 records but were no better than runners-up. The '73 squad was 12-0 and fifth in the national polls. In 1994 Penn State bullied everyone in sight en route to a 12-0 mark capped by a Rose Bowl win over Oregon. Nebraska won the national championship.

Little wonder that Paterno long has been, and remains, a proponent of a Division One football play-off. He believes that the financial bonanza from a college football championship series could help strapped athletic departments to address other concerns, such as fielding equitable programs for men and women.

He thinks it is a disgrace to college football that Division 1A football is the only sport that (the championship) is not decided on the field. All of the other NCAA sports are decided (in play-offs).

Paterno has expressed a willingness to give the current format, the Bowl Championship Series, a chance but still feels that ultimately a play-off is the answer. He struggles with the political nature of the college football polls and puts little stock in the preseason vote which is released before anyone has played a game.

"I don't even pay attention (to polls)," Paterno professed in 1994, saying, "I always sound a little bit exasperated because I don't know how to answer these questions. I don't even think about the darn things. I come to these (press conferences) and all I hear is this nonsense."

On Paterno's watch, Penn State has won two national championships (1982, 1986) and twice lost title games—to Alabama in the 1979 Sugar Bowl and Oklahoma in the 1986 Orange Bowl. After winning his first title with a 27-23 victory over Georgia in the 1983 Sugar Bowl, Paterno professed that he wanted to get off in a corner for a while and remember all the players, the coaches before, who weren't around for this moment.

If we win the national championship, so what? It sounds cornball, but that's the way I feel. Somebody once asked Knute Rockne which team was his best and he said, "The future would determine that." My best team will be the one that produces the best doctors, lawyers, and citizens—not necessarily the one with the best record. Let's keep it in context.[1]

—*Paterno*

~

On advice to a team highly ranked in the preseason:
I told them publicity is like poison. It won't hurt you if you don't swallow it.[2]

—*Paterno*

~

On his opinion of the current method—the Bowl Championship Series—of determining college football's national champion:
The people who have put this thing together are trying very hard to make sure the best two teams get to play one another and do it within the framework of a bowl system they think has to be preserved. There are some of us who disagree. I think in all fairness to them we should see what happens. I would very much prefer a play-off of some sort whether it is four teams or eight teams. I think we should give the BCS a chance to play out for a couple of years and see what happens.[3]

—*Paterno*

On whether he'll see a play-off in his lifetime:
It depends on how long I live. If I live to be 120, maybe.[4]

—*Paterno*

One of the best parts about winning a national championship is that free ride after the game.

On being No. 1:
All of a sudden you go from two to one, and people want to know what kind of a guy Joe Paterno is. You can be number two eight years in a row and nobody cares.[5]

—*Paterno*

On returning to State College following PSU's Sugar Bowl win over Georgia to secure the national championship:
With emergency lights circling, each town's fire engine escorted us up the highway to deliver us to the care of the next town's engines in a hundred-mile relay of joy and pride. I never saw such love between people who didn't know each other. And never in one place at one time have I sensed so many football players in their private darkness sneaking so many silent, exultant tears.[6]

—*Paterno*

A political poll represents a reflection of public sentiment, but football polls are little more than calculated guesses. Very seldom do they end the way they started. They do create interest, but serve no purpose as far as the outcome of the season is concerned.[7]

—*Paterno*

It is a little bit ironic and a little bit hypocritical that the reasons they (the play-off critics) say you can't have a football play-off don't seem to count when you are talking about basketball. I think the basketball play-off is a great thing. I am just amazed that some of those kids can handle their schoolwork and be involved in them, but they obviously do. I think it would be great for college football just as it is great for college basketball.[8]

—*Paterno*

On his undefeated but shunned 1994 team:
Who said we didn't win a championship? The media said we didn't win a championship. We think we won a championship. We did everything we could and we are going to assume we are champions. Not to take anything away from Nebraska but I think this team did everything it could and is certainly a national-championship-caliber football team. We are going to assume that. We are going to treat ourselves as champions, and I am going to treat them as champions.[9]

—*Paterno*

What I owe to my team is to make sure that everybody plays who works hard and has the opportunity to play. For me to not play some kids who have really looked forward to playing on a Saturday because I want to make sure we win by a certain number of points to preserve a place in the rankings would be irresponsible.[10]

—*Paterno*

~

On advice to players about the polls:
I tell them that the media and a lot of other people can take a lot of fun out of the season you are having. You are playing really well, have achieved some things and have games left to play that you should enjoy. Don't get caught up in a lot of talk and debate about something you can't do anything about.[11]

—*Paterno*

~

10

The Press and Media

FOR MEMBERS OF the news media, Joe
Paterno often can be an enigma. If you are
looking for an insightful quote, Paterno will
deliver. He can pronounce witty one-liners,
intuitive commentary, and sharp analysis as
well as anyone. There are occasions,
however, when his media dictates can make
a reporter's work difficult.

Success has increased the media demand on Paterno. So
too has the proliferation of new media—cable sports channels,
sports talk radio, Internet chat sites, and on and on. Press
conferences that used to be attended by five or six souls now
are beamed by satellite to outlets across the nation. Press
attendance at a Nittany Lions home game can reach as high
as five hundred working reporters and broadcasters.

Early in his coaching career, Paterno and Jim Tarman,
the then-sports information director, barnstormed the East
to attract press attention for Penn State football. Their

fervor and Paterno's coaching success were a powerful attraction.

These days, the trick is to manage the media attention, not to attract it. Penn State has become a regular on national television. With that has come an increased focus on everything that happens within the football program. The coach clings to past policies such as closed practices and limits on injury information—unusual in the all-access media climate of the present.

Paterno remains one of the rare coaches to attend a Friday evening social with media covering home and away games. At Indiana in 1994, the media reception turned into a truly memorable event when the Hoosiers' basketball coach, Bob Knight, an old Paterno acquaintance and friend, dropped in. For more than an hour, Knight and Paterno exchanged opinions, one-liners, and coaching advice in a conversation filled with wit and wisdom.

OVER THE LAST THREE DECADES, NOBODY HAS STAYED TRUER TO
THE GAME AND AT THE SAME TIME TRUER TO HIMSELF THAN JOSEPH
VINCENT PATERNO, JOEPA TO PENN STATE WORSHIPPERS—A MAN
SO PATENTLY STUBBORN THAT HE REFUSES TO GIVE UP ON THE
NOTION THAT IF YOU HACK AWAY AT ENOUGH WINDMILLS A FEW OF
THOSE SUCKERS WILL FALL.[1]

—*Rick Reilly, columnist,* Sports Illustrated

JOE PATERNO'S LEGACY ISN'T HIS WON-LOST RECORD AT PENN
STATE. HIS LEGACY IS HIMSELF. HIS IMPACT ON HIS PLAYERS. HIS
INTEGRITY. HIS INSTINCT. HIS GUTS TO DO THE RIGHT THING. THAT
LEGACY DEVELOPED AS EARLY AS THE COACH'S FOURTH SEASON
WHEN HE SUDDENLY WAS SURROUNDED BY THE FLAMES OF A
NATIONAL CONTROVERSY WITH THE PRESIDENT OF THE UNITED
STATES. BUT HE HAS NEVER FLINCHED.[2]

—*Dave Anderson, Pulitzer Prize–winning columnist,* New York Times

PATERNO IS DEMANDING. HE ALWAYS SEEMS TO WANT A LITTLE MORE THAN YOUR BEST AND GETS LOUDLY PERSONAL WHEN THAT DOESN'T HAPPEN. THROW OUT THE MOST POSITIVE VIRTUES— PASSION, LOYALTY, WIT, WARMTH, TENACITY, A BRILLIANT MIND, AND A WORK ETHIC SECOND TO NONE—AND THEY ALL FIT PATERNO. YET HE ALSO CAN BE ABRASIVE, SARCASTIC, JUDGMENTAL, UNBENDING. NOT TO MENTION THAT HAIR-TRIGGER TEMPER THAT FREQUENTLY ERUPTS ON THE SIDELINES AND SOMETIMES GETS CAPTURED ON TELEVISION. USUALLY, SUE GIVES THE MATTER A GOOD AIRING AT HOME, AND JOE APOLOGIZES.[3]

—Ken Denlinger, author and Washington Post *reporter*

CALLING JOSEPH VINCENT PATERNO JUST A FOOTBALL COACH IS LIKE SAYING LEONARDO DA VINCI WAS JUST ANOTHER PAINTER OR WINSTON CHURCHILL WAS JUST ANOTHER POLITICIAN.[4]

—Los Angeles Times

PATERNO IS HEALTHY ENOUGH, SMART ENOUGH TO GO ON COACHING FOR A LONG TIME. WELL PAST THE AGE MOST OTHER COACHES WOULD BE OUT FISHING. PATERNO DOESN'T HUNT OR FISH. HE DOESN'T PLAY GOLF. HIS ENTIRE LIFE IS HIS COACHING JOB, HIS FUND-RAISING FOR THE UNIVERSITY, HIS FAMILY, AND HIS PLAYERS.[5]

—Ron Christ, sports reporter, Harrisburg Patriot

ACCORDING TO THE VALUES WE SHOULD ALL SET FOR OURSELVES, JOSEPH VINCENT PATERNO IS THE MOST DIVINE HUMAN TO EVER COACH COLLEGE FOOTBALL. HE IS THE CONSCIENCE OF THE GAME. HE ONCE SAID "FOOTBALL IS A PART OF LIFE—NOT LIFE."[6]

—*Jim Dent, sports columnist,* San Antonio Express-News

WITHOUT THE DRAMATICS OF ROCKNE, THE IMPERIAL TRAPPINGS OF BRYANT, THE AUTHORITARIANISM OF WOODY HAYES AND THE REST OF THAT OVERBEARING GROUP, IT'S BEEN THE CEREBRAL PATERNO WHO HAS TRIUMPHED OVER TIME AND PLACE. JOE PATERNO THE EDUCATOR WHO HAS BECOME HIS STATE'S LEADING CITIZEN AND THE NATION'S MODEL COACH. PATERNO WHO MAYBE CONCEDED COSMETIC NUANCES AS THE WORLD UNDERWENT UPHEAVAL, YET HELD FIRM TO THE IDEALS HE ESPOUSED, WHO REMAINED UNAFFECTED BY THE ACCOLADES, AS CONSTANT AND UNCHANGING AS THE UNADORNED UNIFORMS HIS TEAMS WEAR.[7]

—*Harvey Yavener, sports reporter,* Trenton Times

AT SEVENTY-THREE, PATERNO'S NOT THAT OLD, AT LEAST COMPARED TO SOME TREES.[8]

—*Tim Cowlishaw,* Dallas Morning News

EVEN THOUGH HE IS ENORMOUSLY SUCCESSFUL AT IT, FROM THE PERSPECTIVE OF MEANINGFUL CONTRIBUTIONS TO SOCIETY, THE LEAST IMPORTANT THING JOE PATERNO DOES IS COACH FOOTBALL.[9]
—*Bill Lyon, sports columnist*, Philadelphia Inquirer

HE EARNED HIS TITLES IN 1982 AND 1986, AND ALSO EARNED SOMETHING IMPORTANT ALONG THE WAY. THE RESPECT OF THE SPORTING WORLD. WHILE THE REST OF COLLEGE FOOTBALL DECAYS AROUND HIM, PATERNO REMAINS A CLASS ACT. HE WINS AND HE DOES IT THE RIGHT WAY. HIS PLAYERS DO NOT TAUNT, STRUT OR DANCE. THEY DO NOT DRESS IN ARMY FATIGUES. THEY DO NOT GO ON SHOPPING SPREES AT FOOT LOCKER WITH A BOOSTER'S CREDIT CARD. THEY MERELY WIN. AND THEY GRADUATE.[10]
—*Jim Caple, sports reporter*, Minneapolis Star and Tribune

When I go to a basketball game, I go nuts because I am coaching, but nobody is paying any attention to me. I am giving all kinds of great advice but nobody listens. The coach is down on the court and involved in it. That's the same way I am with you guys (the press). I am down there and you guys are up there giving me all kinds of advice. And I am not paying any attention to you.[11]
—*Paterno*

Regarding a complimentary 60 Minutes *Paterno segment in 1979:*
WATCHING THE PROGRAM, A FAN MIGHT HAVE ASSUMED THAT
PATERNO IS COACHING 125 WALK-ONS FROM THE PHYSICS
DEPARTMENT, MOST OF WHOM ELECTED TO PLAY AT PENN STATE IN
A NARROW CHOICE OVER HARVARD AND THE SORBONNE.[12]
                                        —*Pete Axthelm, former* Newsweek *columnist*

HE IS AN HONORABLE MAN IN THAT HE PRACTICES WHAT HE
PREACHES—I ALWAYS PUT ASIDE THOSE DETRACTORS. IF THEY HAD
ANYTHING THEY COULD FIND WRONG WITH PENN STATE'S
PROGRAM, YOU CAN BET THAT PENN STATE WOULD HAVE BEEN ON
PROBATION BY THE NCAA A LONG TIME AGO.[13]
                —*Ralph Bernstein, former Associated Press Philadelphia sports editor*

PATERNO CARES. HE CARES ABOUT PENN STATE, ABOUT THE
NCAA, ABOUT THE FUTURE OF COLLEGE SPORTS. IN A PROFESSION
LITTERED WITH TOO MANY CHEATERS AND FAST TALKERS, HE HAS
ALWAYS BEEN A WELCOMED BREATH OF FRESH AIR.[14]
                        —*Paul Attner, sports reporter,* The Sporting News

As often as Paterno has been quoted in the media, rarely has he had to eat his words. Snow? That's another story.

11

Recruiting

PATERNO IS THE preeminent closer in the sport. While others in the coaching profession regard recruiting one of the responsibilities they least enjoy, Paterno looks forward to his visits to living rooms and family rooms across the nation in the quest to attract top football talent to his Nittany Lions program.

"He wasn't like any other recruiter," defensive lineman Bruce Clark recalled in 1976. "He sounded more like a friend. Nothing hard or pressing. He said most guys he gets graduate. I had friends check that out, and it's true. Paterno never cut up other schools like some coaches who came."

Former All-America running back Charlie Pittman said the coach sensed immediately that his parents were not comfortable with the entire recruiting process. "He spent a lot of time with them," Pittman said. "They left very comfortable, feeling that they turned their son over to

someone who was going to take special care of their child."
Years later, Pittman turned his own son, Tony, over to
Paterno for the same care.

One of the recruiting trips that Paterno most remembers
was to Cinnaminson, New Jersey, to visit high school standout
Andre Collins. There were eighteen children in the family
and, Joe said, "While I was speaking with Andre and his
parents, most of them sat on the steps quietly and listened. I
was impressed with how nicely they were dressed and how
well-behaved they were."

Andre wanted to go to Illinois but his mother, Frances,
had other ideas and refused to sign the Illinois grant-in-aid
form. Andre wound up at Penn State, where he was an All-
America linebacker and had a long career in the NFL.

The Cinnaminson visit turned into a bonanza for the
Nittany Lions. Andre was followed to Penn State by brothers
Gerry, Phil, Jason, and Aaron—all of whom played for
Paterno. Asked at one time if he would offer a grant to a
graduating Collins family standout, Paterno said: "I'll wait to
hear from Frances."

JOE HAD STRESSED THAT IF YOU'RE HEARING FROM SCHOOLS SAYING
YOU'LL GO RIGHT IN THERE AND PLAY, THAT'S NOT REALLY A GOOD
IDEA. I LIKED THAT. I REMEMBER THINKING: "THERE'S NO WAY YOU
CAN GO FROM HIGH SCHOOL RIGHT IN AND PLAY AS A FRESHMAN."[1]
                    —*Peg Sacca, mother of quarterbacks John and Tony Sacca*

Regarding the Paternos' honeymoon:
A MONTH OR SIX WEEKS IN EUROPE ENDED UP AS FIVE DAYS
BETWEEN WILLIAMSBURG AND VIRGINIA BEACH—AT THAT TIME,
THERE WERE FEW RESTRICTIONS ON RECRUITING SO ON OUR
HONEYMOON WE BOUGHT SALTWATER TAFFY FOR HIS RECRUITS'
MOTHERS, SENT POSTCARDS TO HIS RECRUITS. IT WAS FINE. IT
BETTER BE FINE. YOU HAVE TO ROLL WITH THE PUNCHES. WHEN
WE GOT HOME FROM THE HONEYMOON, HE LEFT TWO DAYS LATER
WITH (FELLOW ASSISTANT COACH) EARL BRUCE TO GO
RECRUITING. I THOUGHT HE WAS MARRIED TO EARL BRUCE FOR
THE FIRST TWO MONTHS.[2]

                                                            —*Sue Paterno*

It would be "Joe" almost as soon as Marilyn Renkey greeted Paterno and (Tom) Bradley and guided them off the foyer and into a living room mostly used for formal occasions such as this, where her ex-husband was waiting. Comfortable in the company of Presidents of the United States, having been honored by Ronald Reagan at the White House less than a year earlier after Penn State won its second National Championship, Paterno immediately put Marilyn and Mel at ease.[3]

—*Ken Denlinger*, For the Glory

I don't think there's a lot of difference in kids. Their lifestyle has changed in the sense there's more pressure on them. They don't seem as happy. I think they all still want discipline. I think they all want you to be honest with them. They don't like the phonies and they want to be challenged. They want somebody interested in them. They'll respond to love just like kids have done all the time, but then I pick up the paper and some twenty-one-year-old kid commits suicide and I'm saying to myself maybe I'm kidding myself. Maybe there is a big difference, and maybe I have been oblivious to it.[4]

—*Paterno*

IT WAS JUST THAT YOU HAD AN IMMEDIATE TRUST IN HIM. HE'S A REGULAR PERSON. WHEN YOU'RE A HIGH SCHOOL STUDENT YOU GET SO MANY PEOPLE WHO COME IN AND IT'S LIKE THEY'RE SALESMEN. JOE COMES IN AND IT'S LIKE HE'S YOUR UNCLE OR A FRIEND OF THE FAMILY, AND HE'S GENUINELY LIKE THAT.[5]

—*Greg Gattuso, defensive lineman (1981–83)*

IT SEEMED LIKE HE WAS GOING TO TAKE CARE OF ME. AS A PERSON.[6]

—*Bob Jones, defensive lineman (1998–99)*

I THINK JOHN (CAPPELLETTI) SIGNED WITH JOE BECAUSE HE SAW HIM AS A KIND OF SURROGATE FATHER. DAD WAS VERY STRICT WITH US, AND JOE HAD A REPUTATION FOR BEING SOMETHING OF A TASKMASTER. I THINK JOE'S SENSE OF DISCIPLINE APPEALED TO JOHN.[7]

—*Martin Cappelletti, brother of*
Heisman Trophy winner John Cappelletti

It was a hard decision making a choice of colleges. At the time, I didn't know much about it, but I think the one thing that swayed me was the man sitting to my right, and that is Coach Paterno. When I was being recruited, he came down to my house. I think he was not only on a recruiting trip, but he was looking for a good meal—an Italian meal. When he came to the door, he looked over, and on the couch was my brother, Joseph, lying there. He was very ill at the time, more so than usual, and—Coach Paterno was more concerned and talked more about what he could do for my brother than what he could do to get me to Penn State. For this I am very thankful.[8]

—*John Cappelletti,*
Heisman Trophy–winning running back (1971–73)

I realized Joe was coming in behind me. People clean up houses for Joe Paterno. Not for many other coaches. He is a very, very effective recruiter.[9]

—*Anonymous rival coach*

In the old days when you had unlimited visits, you could go out and visit a kid and spend some time in the town. I remember when I was a young assistant coach, you would go in town and stop at the gas station and ask if there was anyone in town worth a look. You can't do that any more because you aren't able to spend as much time on the road.[10]

—*Paterno*

When you watch a kid play in a basketball game, you can see his feet and whether he can control the basketball with his hands. You can see whether he sees people on the court. How he rebounds and if he can jump. How he changes directions if he is playing defense. There are all kinds of things that relate to football you can see on a basketball floor that you probably can't see if you are looking at a tape of a high school game. If we come down to the wire and the staff is just not sure if a kid is good enough, we will watch him play basketball if we have the opportunity. That usually tells us yes or no.[11]

—*Paterno*

IF HE DOESN'T LIKE (THE RECRUIT) AS A PERSON, WE'RE NOT GOING TO RECRUIT HIM. I DON'T CARE HOW GOOD A PLAYER HE IS.[12]

—*Tom Bradley, assistant coach*

12

Pro Football

IN 1973 THE New England Patriots of the National Football League made Paterno one of those offers that can't be refused. He went to bed as coach, general manager, and part owner of the Patriots, only to awaken with the realization that his heart wasn't in it. He called Patriots owner Billy Sullivan, who already had scheduled a press conference to make the announcement, and refused New England's millions.

It was not the first, nor the last time, the NFL has come calling for the services of Penn State's venerable coach. The Baltimore Colts, Pittsburgh Steelers, and New York Giants, among others, all have floated coaching opportunities.

While he has spurned NFL coaching overtures, Paterno has provided a steady stream of outstanding athletes to the professional playing ranks. In his fifty seasons at Penn State, more than 225 of his players have gone on to play in the pros. Twenty-five have been first-round draft choices, including

LaVar Arrington and Courtney Brown of his 1999 team. Three standouts during Paterno's Penn State tenure—Lenny Moore, Franco Harris, and Jack Ham—are enshrined in the Pro Football Hall of Fame in Canton, Ohio.

In a 1995 survey of pro football general managers and personnel directors by *The Sporting News*, Penn State was a clear-cut winner as the college program that best prepares players for the NFL.

On the difference between college and pro football:
It (a college game) is more fun. There is more variation in
the way the game is played. I think that and the whole
campus scene is different from the pro scene. The old
Alums coming back and the enthusiasm that brings makes
it a more exciting situation. That doesn't mean every
college game is better than every pro game or that pro
football is dull. I just think college football is a little bit
more exciting.[1]

—Paterno

On college players leaving early for the professional draft:
If a kid wants to go and is good enough, I think he has
every right to go and nobody should resent it.
Unfortunately, there are going to be people that are going
to try and convince kids that they should go when they are
unprepared both physically and emotionally.[2]

—Paterno

I was having lunch with some friends at the Corner Room one afternoon when the waitress came to the table and said I had a call from a Coach Lombardi. I went to the phone and Vince Lombardi, who I knew from my youth in Brooklyn, said he was getting ready to make his first-round draft choice and wanted to know what I thought about Dave Robinson. I told him I thought Robby was a great college football player, but it was difficult for me to evaluate how he might do on the next level. "Well, the Packers are going to draft him, Joe," Lombardi said to me, "and he had better be good."[3]

—*Paterno*

I really don't pay much attention to anything anybody tells me about the (NFL) draft because it is a little bit like recruiting. I don't think many people know what they are talking about.[4]

—*Paterno*

COACH, I'M READY TO MAKE YOU AN ARRANGEMENT THAT WOULD ENSURE YOUR FAMILY'S WELL-BEING. YOU WOULD NEVER HAVE TO WORRY ABOUT THEM AGAIN.[5]

—*Billy Sullivan, president and owner, New England Patriots*

To his wife after deciding to decline the Patriots'
offer:
You went to bed with a millionaire, but you
woke up with me. I'm not going.[6]

—*Paterno*

~

IF EVER THERE WAS A MAN WHO WOULD TURN
DOWN A MILLION DOLLARS, HE IS THE GUY. YOU
TAKE ONE LOOK AT HIM DRIVING AROUND IN HIS
'65 MUSTANG, AND YOU KNOW HE WOULD
RATHER STICK TO HIS PRINCIPLES THAN TAKE
THE MONEY.[7]

—*John Cappelletti*

~

13

Family

ANGELO PATERNO, JOE'S father, fought Pancho Villa with General John J. Pershing and put himself through law school at night. He died unexpectedly at age fifty-eight in 1955. "Dad was a warm, wonderful human being who always saw the best in people," Paterno said.

"I probably absorbed my shame of losing from my mother," Paterno noted. Florence Paterno, who lived to the age of ninety-two before passing away in 1989, has been described as strong-willed, outspoken, and an extrovert—qualities she obviously passed on to her firstborn.

Joe met his wife, Sue, in the library when he was monitoring study hall for Nittany Lions football players. Their relationship developed as they discovered an increasing number of mutual interests, and they were married in May 1962.

Sue Paterno is an integral part of Joe's life and his career. Together, they constitute a formidable team. Sue has tutored numerous student-athletes, cooked thousands of Italian meals for recruits' parents, University donors, and other distinguished guests, and been a constant source of sound and valuable advice.

"Penn State will replace me," Paterno has offered, "but they'll have a heck of a time replacing Sue."

The Paternos raised five children: Diana, Mary Kay, David, Jay, and Scott, all of them Penn State graduates. They have since been blessed with nine grandchildren.

Since 1969, the Paternos have lived in the same house approximately three blocks from the Penn State campus. Joe often walks to work or to functions in nearby University buildings.

Joe's celebrity has often made it difficult for the family. He is so recognizable that it's difficult for him to appear in public without being besieged by fans. The family once voted to leave him behind rather than endure another amusement park outing with him being followed by admirers of Penn State and the football program.

"My father was not home very often—yet, the little time he spent away from work, he spent with us—not golfing, playing tennis, or even watching television," daughter Mary Kay Hort recalled in a 1998 article.

My mother always said two things. Her parents came over here to be Americans, not Italians, and we never want to forget we're Italians.[1]

—*Paterno*

I THINK MY FAVORITE LESSON FROM MY FATHER DEFINES HIM AND HIS SUCCESS. HANGING IN OUR KITCHEN IS AN UGLY FRAMED SKETCH OF TWO HIPPOS. NEXT TO THE HIPPOS IT SAYS, "IT IS BETTER TO BE HATED FOR WHAT ONE IS, THAN TO BE LOVED FOR WHAT ONE IS NOT." THIS IS HIS PHILOSOPHY. IT IS BETTER TO MAKE TOUGH AND UNPOPULAR DECISIONS THAN TO BE UNTRUE TO ONESELF. HE HAS NEVER BEEN AFRAID TO DO WHAT HE BELIEVES IS THE RIGHT THING, AND NEVER SHRINKS FROM STATING HIS OPINION.[2]

—*Mary Kay Hort, daughter*

DINNER TIMES WERE OUR FAMILY TIME, AND HE MADE SURE WE ALL LEARNED SOMETHING AT EACH MEAL. SOMETIMES IT WAS A LESSON IN TABLE MANNERS OR A CONTEST ABOUT WHO COULD RECITE THE UNITED STATES PRESIDENTS IN ORDER.[3]

—*Mary Kay Hort*

HE'S GOT A LOT OF ENERGY. IT NEVER FAILS TO AMAZE ME. I JUST
HOPE IT'S GENETIC.[4]

—Jay Paterno, son and Penn State assistant coach

JOE DEMANDS SO MUCH OF HIMSELF, HE DRIVES HIMSELF AT A
TERRIBLE PACE. HE THINKS HE CAN BE A GOOD COACH AS LONG AS
HE WORKS HARD AT HIS JOB, AS LONG AS HE PAYS ATTENTION TO
DETAILS, AND HE IS A BUG ON THAT. HE BLAMES HIMSELF WHEN WE
LOSE, THAT HE DIDN'T WORK HARD ENOUGH, THAT HE COULD HAVE
DONE SOMETHING DIFFERENT IF HE HAD PAID ATTENTION TO ONE
MORE LITTLE DETAIL. I THINK HIS BIGGEST FEAR IN LIFE IS
OVERLOOKING A DETAIL.[5]

—Sue Paterno

Dad was a warm, wonderful human being who always saw
only the best in people. He was always himself. Everybody
who ever met him liked him. Dad was easygoing but he had
a way of making you see his point. He liked to talk
politics—he was an avid supporter of Franklin D.
Roosevelt—and we really got into some warm discussions
around the house. Dad was genuinely interested in what all
of us did, and we had a great family relationship.[6]

—Paterno

If we had a classroom spelling bee, I was expected to win it.
I had to be able to do multiplication tables faster than
anyone else. Why? Because of the image in the back of my
head of my mother expecting me to defend my honor—our
family honor. I probably absorbed my shame of losing from
my mother.[7]

—*Paterno*

Forget about your personal life during the season. You don't
have any. You get up early in the morning and look at
tapes. You have staff meetings. I am fortunate that I live
close enough to campus that I can run home and get a bite
to eat. Then you are back looking at tapes and back at a
staff meeting, and it goes on and on.[8]

—*Paterno*

When I was a younger coach, we used to take the kids
down to Hershey to the park when they were small. Then
we started to get some recognition and have some success
and kids would stop me for autographs and things like that.
My kids finally had a vote and said that the next time they
went to Hershey they were going without me.[9]

—*Paterno*

On Sue Paterno:
SHE IS THE BALANCE IN HIS LIFE.[10]

—*Scott Paterno, son*

IT WOULD HAVE BEEN NICE IF HE COULD HAVE GONE TO MORE SPORTING EVENTS, OR PTA MEETINGS, OR OPEN-HOUSE NIGHTS AT SCHOOL, BUT I NEVER FELT THAT I MISSED OUT ON ANYTHING BECAUSE I KNEW HOW MUCH HE CARED ABOUT US.[11]

—*Diana Paterno, daughter*

Sue and Joe Paterno have been Penn State benefactors in more ways than one.

14

Friends and Role Models

A GENIAL PERSONALITY notwithstanding, Joe Paterno is not someone to spend hours on the telephone—to engage in much small talk. His hectic schedule keeps him on the move, an elusive target for friendly banter.

Watching him in a social setting, one can quickly discern that Paterno is unquestionably a people person. He puts strangers at ease and finds a conversational connection whether the respondent is a bell captain or a captain of industry.

His friendships with many of the nation's movers and shakers has been a boon to Penn State's fund-raising effort. The University has no more effective finisher than the affable Paterno, who has not hesitated to be an advocate for development endeavors.

One of Paterno's favorite respites is the off-season coaches trip sponsored by the Nike Corporation, a corporate sponsor of Penn State athletics. It gathers the football coaches of the

Nike-sponsored schools at some exotic port of call where Paterno enthusiastically joins in the fun and games.

Probably no single person had more impact on Paterno's early development than Father Bermingham, a hero to him in every sense of the word. Father Bermingham stimulated Joe's academic curiosity and motivated him to read Virgil's epic poem, the *Aeneid*, in the original Latin.

Another friend and hero for Paterno is assistant coach Jim O'Hora, a member of the Penn State staff when Paterno arrived in 1950. Joe lived with Jim and his wife, Betts, for nine years. By Joe's account, Jim ran interference for him when he was impatient in staff meetings and encouraged and nurtured him as a person.

Jackie Robinson, General George Patton, and Vince Lombardi are among other heroes Paterno has identified. His heroes are not always obvious, but they are almost always uncommon people doing uncommon things.

HOW MANY FOOTBALL COACHES MAJORED IN ENGLISH
LITERATURE AT AN IVY LEAGUE SCHOOL? WHEN HE SITS UP HALF
THE NIGHT, AS HE DID FOR YEARS, DOING 'X'S AND 'O'S FOR THE
NEXT DAY'S PRACTICE OR NEXT SATURDAY'S GAME, HE ALWAYS
LISTENED TO OPERA. I THINK THE FACT THAT HE HAS SUCH A
BROAD RANGE OF INTERESTS IS ONE OF THE REASONS OUR
FOOTBALL PROGRAM IS DIFFERENT.[1]

—*Jim Tarman, former Penn State athletic director*

JOE IS SO MUCH MORE INVOLVED IN PENN STATE THAN JUST THE
FOOTBALL PROGRAM. HE'S INTERESTED IN THE DEVELOPMENT OF THE
STUDENT-ATHLETE AS A WHOLE, AND THE DEVELOPMENT OF PENN
STATE AS A GREAT, GLOBAL UNIVERSITY. HE'S AN ICON FOR PENN STATE
AND WILL CONTINUE TO BE A SYMBOL OF THE BEST OF PENN STATE IF
HE LIVES TO BE 100.[2]

—*Bill Schreyer, chairman emeritus of Merrill Lynch*
and past president of the Penn State board of trustees

HE HAS AN INSTINCT FOR PICKING THE RIGHT MAN FOR THE RIGHT
POSITION. HE HAS THE COURAGE TO EXPERIMENT AND GAMBLE ON
CHANGING A PLAYER'S POSITION IF HE FEELS THAT HE WOULD PLAY
A LITTLE BETTER SOMEWHERE ELSE OR IF THE TEAM WOULD BENEFIT
FROM IT.[3]

—*Sever Toretti, former Penn State assistant coach*

HE'S MADE MISTAKES, BUT I THINK JOE HAS THAT CONFIDENCE
THAT NOBODY IS GOING TO OUTCOACH HIM DURING A GAME.[4]
> —Ridge Riley, former Penn State Alumni Association director

I KNOW THEY WERE CLOSE—RIP HAD A LOT OF RESPECT FOR JOE—I
THINK JOE HAS DONE EVERYTHING FOR PENN STATE, AND MORE.
JOE HAS DONE SO MUCH NOT JUST FOR THE FOOTBALL PROGRAM,
BUT FOR OTHER PARTS OF THE UNIVERSITY. YES, I THINK RIP WOULD
BE DELIGHTED. THERE ARE MANY FOOTBALL COACHES. BUT THERE
WILL NEVER BE ANOTHER ONE LIKE JOE.[5]
> —Sunny Engle, widow of Penn State coach Rip Engle

I'm not a phone guy. I don't get on the phone and talk to
people. There is always something that I think I have to be
doing so I really haven't had the luxury of being the kind
to stay close to friends. Some of the best friends I have in
life and in football I don't really get to talk to very much.[6]
> —Paterno

On his mentor, Father Thomas Bermingham:
We're all products of the people we meet in our life. Father
Bermingham was a great influence.[7]
> —Paterno

On the Yankee Clipper, Joe DiMaggio:
He came up to a game one time, and I said I wanted him to talk to the team. He said, "What would I say to the team, they won't even know who I am." I said, "They will know who you are." He came into the locker room before the game. He got in that locker room and everybody started to get their cameras. He looked around as if to say, "What should I say?" He said, "Fellows, you are young, you have a good team, have some fun." Then he turned to me and said, "Was that OK?" The kids all gave him a round of applause.[8]

—*Paterno*

Every football coach ought to see the movie *Patton*. He had the ability to rally people around a cause, to get them to make greater sacrifices than they thought were possible. He had the ability to get people to do things by the sheer power of his personality, by his drive and his inspirational qualities. In that respect he was fantastic. He paid attention to small details and felt that if you took care of the little things, the big things would take care of themselves. He was a bug on spirit and morale. He believed that he was destined for great things and there was never any doubt in his mind that he would succeed. That's the attitude a football coach must have.[9]

—*Paterno*

On coaching associate Jim O'Hora:
Without Jim O'Hora I never would have survived at Penn State. He fought battles for me, he defended me, he even gave up friendships for me . . . Jim would sit and listen to me while I poured out my heart. He would point out where I was wrong. He encouraged me to be patient.[10]

—*Paterno*

Jackie Robinson was truly a remarkable athlete, but more than all of these extraordinary deeds, in Jackie Robinson's life a voice had become audible. A note had been struck more true and more thrilling, more able to do justice to the restlessness of a race engaged in fighting for its dignity and its God-given rights. That voice is still engaged in the ongoing struggle—its memory remains and its promise of success lingers.[11]

—*Paterno*

15

Presidents and Politics

THE SUCCESSFUL CANDIDATE in the 2000 election will become the eleventh president to occupy the White House since Joe Paterno joined the Penn State coaching staff in the summer of 1950. That's one of the more stunning statistics of Paterno's remarkable tenure—which began in the second year of Harry Truman's first elected term and will continue into the administration of Bill Clinton's successor. A politician should have such staying power.

Politics was dinner-table conversation in Paterno's childhood home where his father Angelo was a disciple of FDR. Paterno has crossed paths with presidents on numerous occasions, including a famous face-off with Richard Nixon over the latter's decision to award the 1969 National Championship to the University of Texas. When Nixon attempted to recover by offering the Nittany Lions a plaque in recognition of the nation's longest winning, and unbeaten, streaks, Paterno suggested the president might make better use of his time.

Paterno has been something of a regular at 1600 Pennsylvania Avenue, but the visit he doubtless enjoyed most was the one when his 1986 National Championship team called on Ronald Reagan and Vice President George Bush. He presented Reagan a No. 1 jersey with, not surprisingly, no name on the back.

Paterno actually played a supporting role in the election of one of the occupants of the Oval Office. In 1988 at the Republican National Convention in the Louisiana Superdome—fittingly the site of Penn State's first National Championship—the Penn State skipper seconded the nomination of ex-Ivy Leaguer George Bush as the Republican nominee. The coach's decision caused a firestorm among Pennsylvania Democrats, which Paterno defused by remarking, "Being a football coach doesn't make me a non-citizen."

Paterno today has the same passion about politics, and its potential for improving the lot of all citizens, that he has for the game he most loves and best understands—college football.

On the occasion of Penn State's White House visit to honor the 1986 team:

AND SPECIAL CONGRATULATIONS TO COACH JOE PATERNO. FOR MY MONEY, I THINK HE'S ONE OF THE GREATEST COACHES EVER IN COLLEGE SPORTS. AND, I'M NOT THINKING JUST OF HIS TWO NATIONAL CHAMPIONS, HIS FOUR TIMES AS COACH OF THE YEAR, HIS FIFTEEN SEASONS IN THE TOP TEN, HIS 80 PERCENT WINNING RECORD, OR HIS LIFETIME TOTAL OF 199 VICTORIES. NO, I SAY HE'S ONE OF THE BEST BECAUSE, WHILE ACCUMULATING ALL OF THOSE HONORS AND RECORDS, HE'S NEVER FORGOTTEN THAT, FIRST AND FOREMOST, HE'S A TEACHER WHO'S PREPARING HIS STUDENTS NOT JUST FOR THE SEASON BUT FOR LIFE.[1]

—Honorable Ronald W. Reagan,
fortieth president of the United States

On President Nixon's declaring Texas national champion over Penn State in 1969:

I'd like to know, how could the president (Richard Nixon) know so little about Watergate in 1973, and so much about college football in 1969.[2]

—Paterno

I AM MOST GRATEFUL FOR YOUR FRIENDSHIP. I LOVE THE GAME. IT
TAUGHT ME A GREAT DEAL AND GAVE ME THE OPPORTUNITY FOR AN
EDUCATION. YOU HAVE DONE A SUPERB JOB IN COACHING BUT MORE
IMPORTANTLY IN BUILDING CHARACTER. IT THRILLS ME TO SEE HOW
EVERYONE LOVES AND RESPECTS YOU.[3]

—Honorable Gerald R. Ford,
thirty-eighth president of the United States

THROUGHOUT HIS TENURE AT PENN STATE, JOE PATERNO HAS LED
HIS NITTANY LIONS IN SMART, AGGRESSIVE, TEAM-ORIENTED
FOOTBALL. AS THEIR PLAIN WHITE JERSEYS AND BLUE NUMBERS
ATTEST, THEY'RE NOT A FLASHY BUNCH. BUT AT THE CONCLUSION
OF EACH COLLEGIATE SEASON, THEY'RE INVARIABLY AMONG THE TOP
TEAMS IN THE COUNTRY. MOST IMPORTANTLY, AT THE END OF THEIR
COLLEGE CAREERS, JOE'S PLAYERS HAVE LEARNED THOSE VALUABLE
LESSONS OF CHARACTER AND MORAL CONDUCT THAT TYPIFY COACH
PATERNO HIMSELF.[4]

—Honorable George H. W. Bush,
forty-first president of the United States

JOE PATERNO IS THE BEST COACH A UNIVERSITY PRESIDENT COULD
EVER HOPE FOR, SETTING AN EXAMPLE OF EXCELLENCE AND
COMMITMENT FOR THE ENTIRE UNIVERSITY. COACH PATERNO IS *MY*
FIRST-STRING QUARTERBACK.[5]

—Dr. Graham Spanier, president of Penn State

As a former college football player himself, President Gerald Ford was one chief executive who could really relate to Paterno.

On seconding the nomination of George Bush:
After a lifetime of being around great competitors, I know
a winner and I know a leader. I know the difference
between bravado and the quiet dignified confidence of a
Joe DiMaggio, of a Walter Payton, of a George Bush.
George Bush will be a great president of the United States
and I humbly second his nomination.[6]

—Paterno

To Julie Nixon Eisenhower at 1987 White House dinner:
It's hard for me to believe I'm here, in the White House,
sitting under a picture of Abraham Lincoln, having
dinner with the president of the United States—me, a
football coach.[7]

—Paterno

*In remarks at the funeral of his father-in-law Hugh Rodham, a
former Nittany Lions football player:*
UNTIL HIS DYING DAY, HE THOUGHT THAT IF THERE WAS A PERFECT
PERSON ON EARTH HIS NAME WAS JOE PATERNO.[8]

*—Honorable William J. Clinton,
forty-second president of the United States*

16

Self-Evaluation

HE'S NOT A person who looks back. For Joe Paterno, the joy is the struggle. Basking in past achievement is for another day. Paterno is able to confine his focus to the next practice—the next game. Don't speak to him about what happened yesterday.

When conversation of a postgame ceremony to mark his three hundredth coaching victory surfaced, Paterno resisted. He wanted, he said, merely to go to the locker room and get ready for the next game. Told that the ceremony was meaningful to the Beaver Stadium faithful, he reluctantly agreed and was moved to tears by the experience.

Paterno, for someone of his stature and celebrity, gets by without a lot of handlers. His daughter helps him with speaking requests, licensing projects, and other opportunities—not some high-powered, big-city agent. He has been known to turn down awards because he did not consider himself a worthy recipient.

He is very selective of the activities with which he agrees to become associated. He is always punctual, though never early, for appointments and is an incessant note taker who frequently answers letters by scrawling a note directly on the stationery of the sender.

A high-profile target for autograph seekers and celebrity watchers, friend Bill Schreyer recounts one story when the tables were turned on the recognizable Paterno during a visit to Schreyer's Jersey shore beach home: "We were out together one Sunday morning, talking away, and all of a sudden some kid spotted him. 'Will you be here on the beach?' he asked Joe. 'I want to go home and get my football. Will you autograph it?'—Word spread and now a whole flock of kids surround him.

"I was getting a little sick of it," Schreyer continued. "After all, it was my house and my beach! Finally, about four houses away this guy comes out, walks down, and says, 'Bill Schreyer! Remember me? I used to work for you in Boston.' I could have kissed the guy!"

Throughout my life, I have always had the ability to concentrate on what has to be done and not worry about things I can't do anything about.[1]

—*Paterno*

I think my top priority in life is to be a good husband and a good father. Then, I hope to be a good influence on the young people with whom I come in contact to be a decent role model for them. I'd like to help them understand that values are important.[2]

—*Paterno*

I'm scared to death to retire, to be frank with you. I don't know what I'd do. I have absolutely no hobbies. I see some of these guys just get out of it before they're ready. I'm not just talking about coaches. They get old fast.[3]

—*Paterno*

As tough as Paterno has been on his coaches and players over the years, he has always been toughest on himself.

One day I came home—and this is a true story—and my neighbor, Betty, called me at 4:30 in the afternoon and said, "Can you help me out, Joe?" I said, "What's the matter?" She said, "I've got a problem. I promised Paul that I was going to have these drapes up by the time he got back from his trip. He's going to be back at 8 o'clock tonight, and I don't know how to get them up." I said, "Betty, show me your problem." So she showed me where the curtain rods were supposed to go, and the drapes, and all that nonsense, and what is supposed to happen, and I said, "Betty, wait a minute, I'll go home and get my tools." So I went home, and my wife Sue said, "Is that you, Joe?" and I said, "Yeah, you better go over to see Betty—she's got a problem."[4]

—Paterno

One thing in life I don't want to be is a hypocrite. I've never had any delusions about myself, the good part and the bad part. I'm not as good as people paint me out to be but I'm not as bad as some people think I am. I've got the appearance that I'm a nice old guy, which I'm not. I can be a mean son-of-a-gun.[5]

—Paterno

I've got a checklist for everything. I've got a checklist for a checklist.[6]

—Paterno

On his habit of sleeping with a pencil and pad in bed:
YOU'RE GOING TO GIVE ME LEAD POISONING FROM THE SHEETS.[7]
                                                    —*Sue Paterno*

~

When the time comes that I don't want to get up and Sue says, "You have to get up, you're the coach," then I will probably get out of it.[8]
                                                    —*Paterno*

~

On personal milestones:
I don't want to sound like a phony but I really don't think much of those things. I am sure I will at some time.[9]
                                                    —*Paterno*

~

On being recognized:
When people come up and say, "Hey Coach, can I have an autograph?" and I'm sitting next to somebody who won a Nobel Prize in physics, I'm embarrassed.[10]
                                                    —*Paterno*

~

This and That

IT MUST BE surprising even to Joe Paterno how much of a public figure Joe Paterno has become.

Mention Penn State—or college football—or integrity in athletics—and a reference to Paterno is sure to follow. He's even been an answer, an incorrect one, on *Who Wants to Be a Millionaire?*

He's been featured on national advertisements for American Express and Burger King and local campaigns for Milano Bread, the Yellow Pages, and spring water. He's appeared on the cover of *Sports Illustrated* and been profiled on *60 Minutes*. He's been photographed by nationally renowned portrait artist Annie Leibovitz and celebrated by presidents of the United States.

You can have a cup of coffee in your very own Joe Paterno mug with your very own six-foot Joe Paterno cutout seated at the table. You can pay for dinner with your special MBNA Joe Paterno credit card.

The man is everywhere in Happy Valley.

The remarkable thing about Joe Paterno is that all of this fanaticism has not changed him one iota. He remains a person of simple needs; a man committed to his job; a devoted husband, father, and grandfather; a loyal friend and a marvelous mentor to the continuing parade of young men who seek his wisdom, discipline, and perspective.

He has won with honor. He has stayed true to his aim to succeed with student-athletes, not merely athletes. He has been resolute to avoid even the hint of impropriety. He has remained modest and unpretentious.

In a day when heroes are in short supply, Joe Paterno is someone to admire.

On being asked to license a Joe Paterno beanie baby doll:
What's a beanie baby?[1]

—Paterno

On the suggestion to publish a book of quotes by and about him:
It'll sell about six copies.[2]

—Paterno

On the Nittany Lions uniforms:
Number one, I don't think our uniforms look that bad. But, I've always been for simple things. There are no stars on the helmet and no names on the jerseys. I guess that says something to kids about team-oriented play and an austere approach to life.[3]

—Paterno

On a Joe Paterno look-alike contest staged by the student body:
I don't know who would want to win it. I sure wouldn't want to win it.[4]

—Paterno

On Joe Paterno cutouts, golf balls, coffee mugs, etc.:
When they wanted me to do them, I said "You're crazy, nobody will buy one of those dumb things." I agreed on the condition that if there was any money to be made it would go to the library. I understand that Joe Paterno's picture is not on a T-shirt because of Joe Paterno. It is there because of Penn State football.[5]

—*Paterno*

Why the white socks:
PATERNO WEARS ATHLETIC SHOES ON THE SIDELINE, SO HE NEEDS TO WEAR THICK ATHLETIC SOCKS. THE SOCKS SHOW SIMPLY BECAUSE PATERNO ALSO ROLLS UP HIS PANTS. WHEN HE WAS MAKING $20,000 A YEAR AND SUPPORTING A WIFE AND FIVE KIDS, HE WANTED TO DRESS IN HIS BEST PANTS FOR WORK, BUT HE DIDN'T HAVE THE MONEY FOR WEEKLY DRY CLEANING. THE HABIT HAS STUCK.[6]

—*Lori Shontz, sports writer*, Pittsburgh Post-Gazette

On who would play his role in a movie biography:
My wife and I talked about that. We thought about Tom Cruise. The only problem was Sue wasn't going to let Julia Roberts play her.[7]

—*Paterno*

On former Notre Dame coach Lou Holtz:
Lou has made a lot of money for me by going on
commercials with me.[8]

—*Paterno*

On the use of fans to keep your players cool:
It's fine to sit under a fan to get cool but then you have to
get up and it's hot. It is all psychological. I don't think it
has any bearing whatsoever—I feel if we have to have a fan
to make us play well, we aren't ready for the game anyway.[9]

—*Paterno*

On the Big Ten Conference:
I think the Big Ten is the best football-playing conference
in the country. We have been fortunate to play some other
teams from other conferences. I just think that when you
look at the first-round draft picks or when you take a look
at the kind of talent that is in the NFL—that if it (the Big
Ten) is not the strongest, it is certainly as strong as any
conference.[10]

—*Paterno*

On the whereabouts of those famous whale pants he wore in 1982:
They are in my closet. I am afraid to try them on. Maybe one of these days I will have a little fun and wear them again. I still have them.[11]

—*Paterno*

~

On qualifications for the Heisman Trophy:
Somewhere they are going to have to redefine what they mean by the Heisman Trophy winner. Is it the best football player in America—the most hyped football player in America—the guy with the most stats? What is it? Who is eligible? Do you have to be a quarterback or a running back or forget about it? Those are the things that people who vote should think about.[12]

—*Paterno*

~

On second thought, let's keep those whale pants hidden away!

On reaction to an Internet site devoted to pets named in his honor:
It depends on what kind of pets they named after me. My nickname used to be the Rat, way, way back.[13]

—*Paterno*

On broadcasting a spring game with his brother and radio analyst George Paterno:
It gave me a great opportunity to let the public know that one Paterno knows what he is doing.[14]

—*Paterno*

To be a successful leader you must have a genuine concern for people and their ability to trust you. Building a team and being a leader starts with your own personal integrity. It's up to you to make it happen. True success occurs if your values and your integrity have prevailed. That is true success and that defines excellence.[15]

—*Paterno*

Endnotes

Chapter 1: Brooklyn and Brown

1. *The Paterno Legacy*, Birmingham, Ala.: Epic Sports, 1997, 16.
2. Ibid., 29.
3. Ibid., 35.
4. Ibid., 30.
5. George Paterno, *Joe Paterno: The Coach from Byzantium*. Champaign, Ill.: Sagamore Publishing, 1997, 5.
6. Ibid., 12.
7. Ibid., 17.
8. Merv Hyman and Gordon White, *Football My Way*. New York: The Macmillan Company, 1971, 73.
9. Ibid., 72.
10. Remarks, National Football Foundation and Hall of Fame Dinner, December 9, 1997.
11. Michael O'Brien, *No Ordinary Joe*. Nashville, Tenn.: Rutledge Hill Press, 1998, 13.
12. Ibid., 19.
13. Ibid., 25.
14. Ibid., 32.
15. Penn State Football Media Guide, 1997, 133.
16. O'Brien, 38.

Chapter 2: Penn State

1. Joe Paterno with Bernie Asbell, *Paterno: By The Book*. New York: Random House, 1989, 170.
2. Ibid., 68.
3. Penn State Intercom, January 22, 1998.
4. Press Conference, September 8, 1998.

5. O'Brien, 62.
6. Ibid., 63.
7. Penn State Football Media Guide, 1995, 128.
8. Ibid., 128.
9. *Philadelphia Daily News*, December 21, 1994, 86.
10. Ibid., 87.
11. Penn State Football Media Guide, 1999, 146.
12. Press Conference, October 16, 1990.
13. *The Paterno Legacy*, 158.
14. Press Conference, November 4, 1997.
15. Press Conference, August 14, 1997.

Chapter 3: College Athletics and Academics
1. *Football News* Interview, September 12, 1989
2. Paterno and Asbell, 17.
3. *Paterno Legacy*, 16.
4. Press State Football Media Guide, 1992, 125.
5. Press Conference, April 26, 1997.
6. Press Conference, April 26, 1997.

Chapter 4: Coaches and Coaching
1. Press Conference, January 3, 1995.
2. Press Conference, January 2, 1993.
3. Ken Denlinger, *For the Glory*. New York: St. Martin's Press, 1994, 142.
4. Gettysburg College Commencement Address, June 3, 1979.
5. Acceptance Remarks, National Football Foundation and Hall of Fame Dinner, December 10, 1991.
6. *Centre Daily Times*, August 15, 1999.
7. *Los Angeles Times*, August 1998.
8. Ibid.

9. *Philadelphia Inquirer*, August 16, 1998.
10. Town and Gown Football Annual, August 1998.
11. Press Conference, October 20, 1998.
12. Press Conference, September 9, 1998.
13. Press Conference, September 15, 1998.
14. Press Conference, August 13, 1998.
15. Hyman and White, 54.
16. O'Brien, 40.
17. Author's Recollection.
18. *The Paterno Legacy*, 38.
19. Press Conference, April 20, 1996.
20. Press Conference, August 14, 1995.
21. Press Conference, December 3, 1994.
22. O'Brien, 184.
23. O'Brien, 191.

Chapter 5: Football
1. Penn State Football Media Guide, 1988, 74.
2. Penn State Commencement Address, June 16, 1973.
3. Press Conference, January 2, 1992.
4. Press Conference, October 22, 1991.
5. Press Conference, October 8, 1991.
6. Hyman and White, ix.
7. Ibid., 16.
8. Ibid., 22.
9. Ibid., 31.
10. Press Conference, November 2, 1999.
11. Press Conference, October 12, 1999.
12. Press Conference, September 10, 1996.
13. Press Conference, October 24, 1995.
14. Press Conference, November 4, 1997.

15. Press Conference, October 14, 1997.
16. Press Conference, September 16, 1997.
17. Press Conference, September 27, 1994.
18. O'Brien, 146.
19. Penn State Football Media Guide, 1989, 85.

Chapter 6: Game Day
1. Mickey Bergstein, *Penn State Sports Stories and More.* Harrisburg, Pa.: RB Books, 1998, 142.
2. Denlinger, 120.
3. Penn State Commencement Address, June 16, 1973.
4. Press Conference, September 8, 1998.
5. *Tampa Tribune*, December 27, 1998.
6. Hyman and White, 25.
7. Paterno and Asbell, 103-4.
8. Press Conference, October 3, 1995.
9. Press Conference, September 30, 1997.
10. Press Conference, August 30, 1994.
11. O'Brien, 172.
12. O'Brien, 183.

Chapter 7: The Players
1. Introductory Remarks, Canton, Ohio, 1990.
2. Denlinger, 303.
3. Penn State Football Media Guide, 1989, 75.
4. Ibid., 76.
5. *Pittsburgh Post-Gazette*, January 25, 2000.
6. *Cedar Rapids Gazette*, October 9, 1999.
7. *Milwaukee Journal-Sentinel*, September 3, 1999.
8. *Blue-White Illustrated*, September 8, 1998.
9. *Blue-White Illustrated*, September 8, 1998.

10. Town and Gown Football Annual, 1998,
11. Steve Halvonik with John Cappelletti, *Cappelletti Penn State's Iron Horse*. Birmingham, Ala.: Epic Sports, 1998, 36.
12. Hyman and White, 12.
13. Press Conference, October 5, 1999.
14. O'Brien, 55.
15. Penn State Football Media Guide, 1995, 131.
16. *Long Beach Press-Telegram*, December 29, 1994.
17. Press Conference, August 27, 1997.
18. O'Brien, 159.
19. O'Brien, 181.
20. Ibid., 184.
21. *USA Today*, April 7, 2000.

Chapter 8: Winning and Losing

1. *Los Angeles Times* Interview, December 28, 1989.
2. Paterno and Asbell, 273.
3. Ibid., 15.
4. Press Conference, August 13, 1998.
5. Penn State Football Media Guide, 1988, 74.
6. Penn State Commencement Address, June 16, 1973.
7. Press Conference, November 10, 1998.
8. Hyman and White, 26.
9. Ibid., 27.
10. Ibid., 27.
11. O'Brien, 24.
12. Press Conference, October 8, 1996.
13. Press Conference, October 8, 1996.
14. Press Conference, January 2, 1997.

Chapter 9: National Championships, Polls, and Publicity
1   *The Paterno Legacy*, 19.
2. Hyman and White, 13.
3. Press Conference, November 9, 1999.
4. Press Conference, November 9, 1999.
5. O'Brien, 103.
6. Ibid., 119.
7. *The Paterno Legacy*, 63.
8. Press Conference, March 21, 1995.
9. Press Conference, January 3, 1995.
10. Press Conference, September 9, 1997.
11. Press Conference, November 1, 1994.

Chapter 10: The Press and Media
1. *Sports Illustrated*, December 1986.
2. *The Paterno Legacy*, Epic Sports, 1997, 15.
3. Denlinger, 303.
4. *Los Angeles Times*, December 1989.
5. *Harrisburg Patriot-News*, January 20, 2000.
6. *San Antonio Express-News*, December 20, 2000.
7. *Trenton Times*, December 30, 1999.
8. *Dallas Morning News*, December 30, 1999.
9. *Philadelphia Inquirer*, March 17, 1999.
10. *Minneapolis Star and Tribune*, January 1995.
11. Press Conference, August 3, 1996.
12. O'Brien, 230.
13. O'Brien, 243.
14. O'Brien, 283-84.

Chapter 11: Recruiting
1. Denlinger, 22.
2. Ibid., 62.

3. Ibid., 31.
4. Penn State Football Media Guide, 1988, 74.
5. *Milwaukee Journal-Sentinel*, September 3, 1999.
6. *Akron Beacon-Journal*, October 2, 1998.
7. Halvonik and Cappelletti, 23.
8. O'Brien, 57.
9. O'Brien, 166.
10. Press Conference, August 12, 1996.
11. Press Conference, September 16, 1997.
12. O'Brien, 164.

Chapter 12: Pro Football
1. Press Conference, September 24, 1991.
2. Penn State Football Media Guide, 1989, 82.
3. Author's Recollection.
4. Press Conference, April 24, 1999.
5. O'Brien, 89.
6. Paterno and Asbell, 12.
7. O'Brien, 94.

Chapter 13: Family
1. *The Paterno Legacy*, 23.
2. Town and Gown Football Annual, 1998.
3. Ibid.
4. Ibid.
5. Hyman and White, 60.
6. Ibid., 62.
7. O'Brien, 6.
8. Press Conference, October 31, 1995.
9. Press Conference, October 14, 1997.
10. O'Brien, 254.
11. O'Brien, 255.

Chapter 14: Friends and Role Models
1. Football Media Guide, 1999, 150.
2. Town and Gown Football Annual, August 1998.
3. Hyman and White, 57.
4. O'Brien, 99-100.
5. *The Paterno Legacy*, 45.
6. Press Conference, September 9, 1997.
7. *The Paterno Legacy*, 29.
8. Press Conference, December 12, 1998.
9. Hyman and White, 48.
10. Ibid., 88-89.
11. Remarks, National Football Foundation and Hall of Fame Dinner, December 9, 1997.

Chapter 15: Presidents and Politics
1. Remarks, The White House, February 2, 1987.
2. Penn State University Commencement Address, June 16, 1973.
3. Denlinger, 39.
4. Acceptance Remarks, National Football Foundation and Hall of Fame Dinner, December 10, 1991.
5. Town and Gown Football Annual, August 1998.
6. Seconding Speech, Republican National Convention, August 18, 1988.
7. O'Brien, 268.
8. *Tri-County Sunday Times*, April 11, 1993.

Chapter 16: Self-Evaluation
1. Press Conference, October 6, 1992.
2. Penn State Football Media Guide, 1987, 63.
3. Denlinger, 305.
4. Gettysburg College Commencement Address, June 3, 1979.

5. *USA Today*, September 8, 1989.
6. O'Brien, 144.
7. Ibid., 144.
8. Press Conference, November 19, 1996.
9. Press Conference, December 3, 1994.
10. *Pittsburgh Tribune-Review*, June 27, 1999.

Chapter 17: This and That
1. Author's Recollection.
2. Author's Recollection.
3. Penn State Football Media Guide, 1997, 62.
4. Penn State Football Media Guide, 1988, 74.
5. Press Conference, August 6, 1991.
6. *Pittsburgh Post-Gazette*, September 11, 1998.
7. *Altoona Mirror*, December 25, 1994.
8. Press Conference, November 19, 1996.
9. Press Conference, September 3, 1996.
10. Press Conference, August 3, 1996.
11. Press Conference, November 25, 1997.
12. Press Conference, October 7, 1997.
13. Press Conference, September 16, 1997.
14. Press Conference, April 26, 1997.
15. Mark Luchinsky Memorial Lecture, March 23, 2000.